Crosscurrents / MODERN CRITIQUES

Harry T. Moore, *General Editor*

American Poems

A CONTEMPORARY COLLECTION

EDITED BY *Jascha Kessler*

WITH A PREFACE BY *Harry T. Moore*

SOUTHERN ILLINOIS UNIVERSITY PRESS
Carbondale and Edwardsville

FEFFER & SIMONS, INC.
London and Amsterdam

Copyright © 1964 by Southern Illinois University Press
All rights reserved
First published, March 1964
Second printing, September 1966
Third printing, December 1969
Printed in the United States of America
Designed by Andor Braun
Standard Book Number 8093–0119–9
Library of Congress Catalog Card Number 64–10627

PREFACE

JASCHA KESSLER'S ANTHOLOGY of American poets under forty is one of the seven books dated Spring 1964 which take this Crosscurrents series into its second dozen of volumes. As in the case of the other items, we are delighted to have Mr. Kessler's book on the list.

By we I mean not only myself but Mr. Vernon Sternberg, Director of Southern Illinois University Press. The series was entirely his idea. I can't remember our first talks about it but can recall his enthusiasm and my own mild skepticism. He insisted that good books about authors of quality, and about literary movements, would sell. Time has proved him right, for most of the books have, as they say, moved very well, and several have achieved second printing.

The first volumes were scheduled for the spring of 1962. How does one get such a series going?

One is always fortunate if he has talented friends. In 1960, Frederick J. Hoffman, who had recently gone to a new professorship at the University of California, Riverside, was asked whether he would undertake a volume, and he offered to write one on Samuel Beckett. Sir Richard Rees, a frequent visitor to Southern Illinois, was approached about a book on George Orwell, who had been one of his closest friends; somewhere out on the Hebrides they had even been associated in managing an animal farm. Meanwhile, two manuscripts came in to us unsolicited: John L. Mersereau's on Mikhail Lermontov and Edward A. and Lillian D. Bloom's on Willa Cather. And I decided to put together a critical and biographical miscellany devoted to an author who had recently come into public view with an exciting tetralogy: Lawrence Durrell. This book for the most part contained material already published, by Lionel Trilling, Carl Bode, Derek Stanford, Gerald Sykes, Henry Miller, Richard Aldington, Bonamy Dobrée, and others. Upon request, Lander Mac-Clintock, an authority on Pirandello, read Durrell's plays and wrote an essay on them; and in a surprisingly rapid time, Victor Brombert prepared a thorough survey of Durrell's critical reputation in France, where he had been taken up with even greater enthusiasm than in English-speaking countries. But our most helpful contributor was Durrell himself, who supplied some interesting letters which had been written to him and permitted us to publish part of his important and interesting correspondence with an editor.

Then, in the spring of 1962, these first five books appeared. Reviewers gave them a generally friendly reception, though none of the volumes was noticed by such media as the New York Times Book Review, which apparently do not review volumes in series. (The Saturday Review, however, has dealt with some of the subsequent books.) Papers in Chicago and other cities reviewed the series, and the Reporter provided a long discussion of Richard Rees's George Orwell: Fugitive from the Camp of Victory.

The Orwell, Durrell, and Beckett books sold well, as we had expected. The volume on Lermontov lagged in sales; this surprised us because of the current interest in Slavic studies and because Lermontov, though dead for more than a century, is so much a hero of our own time, and an influence on writers as diverse as Joyce and Pasternak. That the Lermontov book has moved slowly is no reflection upon its quality. A university press is not a commercial publishing house and doesn't pretend to live off profits, however pleasant they are when they come in. Anyhow, in university-press thinking generally, there's not the same attitude to quality in relation to quantity as there usually is in commercial publishing. Mr. Mersereau's book remains a good one; Mr. Sternberg and I have been somewhat disappointed that more readers haven't so far found their way to it. On the other hand, we were pleasantly surprised at the response to Willa Cather's Gift of Sympathy. We hadn't realized that Willa Cather's literary reputation was quite so good as it apparently is. The fact that Mr. and Mrs. Bloom wrote so excellent a book about this author is also a major factor in its success. The volume has now gone into a second printing.

After the appearance of the first five Crosscurrents titles, manuscripts began to come in and writers began to send inquiries as to possibilities. I established a procedure in relation to future titles by consulting Mr. Sternberg in every case and making no commitments without his approval. This has, for me at least, been a most pleasant working relationship: Mr. Sternberg's advice at all times sound and his coöperation genial. I may add that the books—consider the one you are reading from—are beautifully designed by one of the outstanding men in this field, Andor Braun.

Mr. Braun had four more sets of volumes ready to glow in the bookstores in the autumn of 1962. The College Novel in America, by John O. Lyons, was a rather unusual item, the first book ever written on this subject; and it has attracted a great many interesting comments. Charles Shapiro's Theodore Dreiser: Our Bitter Patriot, was immediately and widely recognized as a superior book on that author; at the time this is being written, Mr. Shapiro's volume has just gone into a second printing. The other two excellent volumes published in 1962 unfortunately had somewhat similar names, and this may have caused a bit of confusion. The two manuscripts were ready at the same time, and we decided to bring the books out simultaneously rather than ask one of the authors to wait a season for the appearance of a book he had prepared for us. My prefaces tried to make it clear that William Van O'Connor's The Grotesque: An American Genre is an altogether different kind of work from Irving Malin's New American Gothic. Reviews across the country helped emphasize the distinction: Mr. O'Connor's book deals with various phases of past and present American literature, and Mr. Malin's with a number of newer writers such as James Purdy and John Hawkes, who have not previously received critical surveys in books.

By this time—fall 1962—sales figures were gratifying indeed. And more unsolicited manuscripts were arriving than could be published. A number of them were rejected, along with some suggested projects which didn't seem to fit into the series. I refused, for example, to consider a book on W. Somerset Maugham on the grounds that he is a gentleman-in-the-parlor entertainer and not exactly pertinent for serious consideration by a university press. In another case I expressed some doubt as to whether to include a certain other item in the series, but asked the author to let me see the manuscript anyhow. He sent it instead to another university press which published the book, and it received good reviews, though perhaps it would have sold more copies as part of our series. We should have had that one; you can't catch them all.

But we were glad to have, for the spring of 1963, the three titles we did publish: Eric Thompson's T. S. Eliot: The Metaphysical Perspective, Charles I. Glicksberg's The Tragic Vision in Twentieth-Century Literature, and Frederick R. Karl's C. P. Snow: The Politics of Conscience. By this time there were many books on Eliot, but this didn't mean there wasn't room for Mr. Thompson's very good one, which dealt with special aspects of his subject, including the first thorough examination of Eliot's unpublished Harvard doctoral thesis on the metaphysics of F. H. Bradley, as well as particularly valuable studies of The Waste Land and "Burnt Norton." Mr. Glicksberg's volume made an excellent sequel to a book which had been brought out by a commercial publisher a year or so before: George Steiner's The Death of Tragedy. Mr. Steiner had dealt only briefly with ancient tragedy and had spent most of his space on neo-classic and romantic examples of the genre, merely touching on the more recent phases; Mr. Glicksberg's considered and expert look at present-day tragedy was very welcome, and an encouraging number of readers indeed welcomed it. Frederick Karl, who has written frequently on current British literature and is now editing Conrad's Complete Letters, wrote for us the first full-size book on C. P. Snow, a temperate estimate of him as a novelist, a tone I tried to reflect in my preface, which like Mr. Karl's book paid little attention to F. R. Leavis's characteristically abusive and cruel attack on Snow. At a book fair shortly after our book appeared, Mr. Sternberg met Sir Charles, and I was delighted because he inscribed a copy of the book for me with thanks for "an introduction which seems to me just about right for an author in his own life-time." Amusingly enough, one of our scientific colleagues at the University, who has a special quarrel with Snow, "reviewed" the book under the headline, "C. P. SNOW HAS NO RIGHT TO SPEAK FOR SCIENCE!" Obviously, the review which prompted that headline had nothing to do with Frederick Karl's book and, in its Catonian attack, actually said nothing about the book. But, Delanda est Cartago, at any cost.

In the autumn of 1963, we came up with five more titles. Undaunted by the lack of response to our volume on Lermontov, we launched F. M. Dostoevsky: Dualism and Synthesis of the Human Soul, by Temira Pachmuss. There are various books on Dostoevsky in English, but few of them which draw upon so many little-known Russian and Western European sources in creating a new and valuable interpretation of one of the greatest, if not the greatest, of all novelists. We were also pleased to bring out Glenn S. Burne's Remy de Gourmont: His Ideas and Influence in England and America, the first full-size book in English on de Gourmont, a critic who is now being revaluated. As Mr. Burne convincingly shows, de Gourmont in his time was a germinal influence on T. S. Eliot, Ezra Pound, Richard Aldington, Kenneth Burke, and other potentially important writers.

That autumn 1963 list also included a thorough study of Shaw's plays by Homer E. Woodbridge; we are sorry that he has not lived on to see his book in print, especially in the handsome design Andor Braun has given it. In The New University Wits and the End of Modernism, William Van O'Connor—the first author to appear twice in the series—deals with the group of postwar English writers usually called, or miscalled, the Angries; Mr. O'Connor places these writers (including Kingsley Amis, Iris Murdoch, Thom Gunn, and John Wain) in a new perspective and provides an important critical survey of the "movement." My preface, written in November 1962, said that England had lost its empire because of outside historical forces and not, as usual, because of inner moral collapse. I was of course using the word moral in the larger sense, and not in any intension that could be applied to a scandal which broke out soon afterward. After all, when England was at the fullness of her power, cabinet ministers, if not kings themselves, often had popsies.

Not least on the fall 1963 list, George Wickes's Henry Miller and the Critics is a judicious selection of writings about Miller by Edmund Wilson, Aldous Huxley, Lawrence Durrell, and others, with a postscript by Miller and excerpts from the testimony of Mark Schorer and Harry Levin at the legal proceedings against Tropic Cancer in Boston in 1961. It is a very full, many-sided book on Miller.

And now, in the present season, spring 1964, the Crosscurrents series offers seven titles, including our first poetry anthology and our first revised edition of a book published earlier elsewhere. The other five volumes are along the more "normal" lines of the series. One of them is a collection of literary essays by Salvatore Quasimodo, the first Nobel Prize winner to have a full book in Crosscurrents; Quasimodo is ably translated by Thomas G. Bergin and Sergio Pacifici, from the second of whom we hope one day to have a book on modern Italian literature.

When the series started, I asked two authors for manuscripts, and at last these are being published. Norman Friedman had written so perceptively about various phases of e. e. cummings (who had his name legally decapitalized) that I suggested he do a rounded study of cummings for us, and it is gratifying to see this excellent book appear. The other volume done by request is Joseph Prescott's Exploring James Joyce, about which I approached its author in 1960 at the Liège conference of the Fédération International des Langues at Littératures Modernes. I was familiar with my friend Mr. Prescott's textual studies of the Joyce manuscripts, particularly of Ulysses, studies which had been scattered through various journals and books; to bring them together in a single volume seemed to me a service to modern readers, since no more valuable explorations of the Joyce material had been undertaken. It is only fair to explain, as in the preface to the Prescott volume, that the title Exploring James Joyce was not Mr. Prescott's idea. He probably considers it a bit dramatic. But, in the Aspern papers-scholar adventurers way of things, his explorations are dramatic.

John Enck, in Wallace Stevens: Images and Judgments, has rescued one of the best modern poets from fragmentary and partial approaches and has presented a coherent and well-rounded view of Stevens' accomplishment. With Ben F. Stoltzfus's searching appraisal of Alain Robbe-Grillet, Crosscurrents gets into avant-garde European literature and presents the first book, in English at least, one of the most exciting participants in the most exciting Continental literary movement of recent years.

The revised edition of After the Genteel Tradition, edited by Malcolm Cowley, brings back a book originally published in 1937 but especially valuable now as the only broad collective study of a number of American writers of the early twentieth century (including Dreiser, Hemingway, Anderson, O'Neill, Dos Passos and others), and examined by such critics as Trilling, Bishop, Cantwell, Arvin, and Mr. Cowley himself. The book not only demonstrates that literary criticism in the 1930s was far better than many readers remember—even brilliant—but

*the volume also stands up with the best of modern criti-
cal ensembles. The Crosscurrents series will not contain
many reprints, but occasionally a revised edition of so fine
a book as* After the Genteel Tradition *will justify such
activity.*

And now for the present book, Jascha Kessler's American Poems: A Contemporary Collection, in which poets
under forty are represented. Mr. Kessler chose sixteen of
them (I am glad he included himself), ranging from
writers as diverse as John Hollander and Allen Ginsberg.
Although limited by space, Mr. Kessler fortunately gave
each poet good representation, which was better than including thirty-two or forty-eight poets with one or two
samples apiece. Getting up a collection of this kind is an
agony, what with all the correspondence and permissions
involved, and I am happy to say that Mr. Kessler is nicely
recovering in the salubrious climate of Perugia. The reason
that, instead of writing a full preface to his book, I have
presented the history of Crosscurrents is that Mr. Kessler
has himself written the best possible introduction to his
collection, and good introduction-wine needs no preface-
bush. So, now that I've placed his book in the Crosscurrents series, I'll let him speak about the book itself,
and I will add only that I think it is a first-rate anthology
which proudly represents an important group of younger
American poets.

HARRY T. MOORE

Southern Illinois University
October 19, 1963

Note

When I wrote the foregoing Preface to Jascha Kessler's
poetry anthology, this book was the twenty-fourth we
had published in the Crosscurrents/Modern Critiques
series whose history I discussed in that Preface. In the
succeeding years the series has tripled in size, and we are
happy to be reprinting still another edition of Mr. Kessler's valuable collection.

December 1969   H. T. M.

ACKNOWLEDGMENTS

PREVIOUSLY PUBLISHED POEMS in this collection are noted below and acknowledgment is made to the poets and publishers for their kind permission to reprint the poems. Other poems in this volume have not been previously published. To those poets who graciously permitted their poems to be published here for the first time the editor and publishers make grateful acknowledgment.

ROBERT CREELEY: "The Rhyme," "I Know a Man," "The Death of Venus," "A Form of Adaptation," "Naughty Boy," "A Form of Women," "Oh No," "A Wicker Basket," "The Wind," "Ballad of the Despairing Husband," "The Invoice," "The End of the Day," "The Wife"; reprinted with the permission of Charles Scribner's Sons from *For Love Poems 1950 - 1960*, by Robert Creeley. Coypright © 1962, by Robert Creeley.

IRVING FELDMAN: "The Ark," "Wrack," "Greenwich Village Saturday Night," "The Hand," "Assimilation," "The Lost Language"; from *Works and Days*, copyright © 1961, Little, Brown and Company, and André Deutsch Ltd.; reprinted by permission of the publishers.

S. S. GARDONS: "Fourth of July," "The Survivors," are reprinted by permission from *The Hudson Review*, Vol. XII, No. 4, Winter 1959 - 60; copyright © 1960 by the Hudson Review, Inc.

ALLEN GINSBERG: "Kaddish," from *Kaddish and Other Poems* (City Lights Books); copyright © 1961, by Allen Ginsberg; reprinted by permission of the publisher.

BARBARA GUEST: "The Hero Leaves His Ship," "Les Réalités," "Sadness," "Belgravia," "The First of May," "Wave," copyright © 1962 by Doubleday & Company, Inc.; from *Poems*; reprinted by permission of the publisher.

JOHN HOLLANDER: "By the Sea," from *A Crackling of Thorns*, by John Hollander; copyright © 1958, by Yale University Press, Inc.; reprinted by permission of the publisher; "Digging It Out," "Slepying Long in Greet Quiete Is Eek a Nourice to Leccherie" from *Movie-Going and other poems*, by John Hollander; copyright © 1962, reprinted by permission of Atheneum Publishers.

JASCHA KESSLER: "My Grandmother's Funeral," appeared in *Midstream*, published by the Theodor Herzl Foundation, New York; "High Summer," reprinted by permission from *New Mexico Quarterly*, copyright © 1962, by the University of New Mexico Press; "Requiem for An Abstract Artist," appeared originally in *Poetry: A Magazine of Verse*.

KENNETH KOCH: "Geography," "Taking a Walk With You," "Aus Einer Kindheit," "The Artist," "The Escape from Hydra," from *Thank You and Other Poems*, by Kenneth Koch, published by Grove Press, Inc., copyright © 1962 by Kenneth Koch. Reprinted by permission of the author.

PHILIP LEVINE: "The Sierra Kid," "Gangrene," appeared originally in *Poetry: A Magazine of Verse*; "Small Game," appeared originally in *Midland*, Random House, 1961; "Passing Out," appeared originally in *The Paris Review*; all are reprinted by permission of the author.

JOHN LOGAN: "Achilles and The King," "Honolulu and Back," "A Trip to Four or Five Towns," from *Ghosts of the Heart*, published by The University of Chicago Press, copyright © 1960, by John Logan.

W. S. MERWIN: "Eleven Poems," appeared originally in *Poetry: A Magazine of Verse*, in January, 1962, and are reprinted with the permission of the author.

ROBERT MEZEY: "The Funeral Home," "The Visit," "Against Seasons," "To Philip Levine: On The Day of Atonement"; from *The Lovemaker,* by Robert Mezey; copyright © 1961, by Robert Mezey; Selections reprinted by permission of the publisher, The Cummington Press, Iowa City, Iowa; "No Country You Remember" appeared originally in *Harper's Magazine.*

W. D. SNODGRASS: "Heart's Needle, 2, 6, 9, 10," from *Heart's Needle,* by W. D. Snodgrass; copyright © 1959, Alfred A. Knopf, printed by permission of the publisher, and The Marvell Press, Ltd., England; "Mementoes ii," reprinted by permission from *The Hudson Review,* Vol. XIII, No. 1, Spring 1960; copyright © 1960 by W. D. Snodgrass; "Leaving Ithaca," reprinted by permission from *The Hudson Review,* Vol. XIII, No. 1, Spring 1960, copyright © 1960 by The Hudson Review, Inc.; "A Flat One," appeared originally in *The Quarterly Review of Literature,* Vol. X, No. 3; "Manet: The Execution of the Emperor Maximilian," reprinted by permission from *The Hudson Review,* Vol. XVI, No. 2, Summer 1963; copyright © 1963 by The Hudson Review, Inc.

JAMES WRIGHT: "At The Executed Murderer's Grave," "The Cold Divinities," copyright © 1958, by James Wright, reprinted from *Saint Judas,* by James Wright, by permission of Wesleyan University Press; "At the Slackening of the Tide," "The Accusation," copyright © 1959, by James Wright, reprinted from *Saint Judas,* by James Wright, by permission of Wesleyan University Press; "A Blessing," "Two Hangovers," "Two Poems about President Harding," copyright © 1961, by James Wright, reprinted from *The Branch Will Not Break,* by James Wright, by permission of Wesleyan University Press; "A Message Hidden in an Empty Wine Bottle," "Stages On a Journey Westward," copyright © 1962, by James Wright, reprinted from *The Branch Will Not Break,* by James Wright, reprinted by permission of the Wesleyan University Press.

CONTENTS

IN THE WILDERNESS
AN UNCRITICAL INTRODUCTION

LOOKING STEADILY at the scene before us and trying to see it whole, one is not really surprised at finding a landscape in moil and turmoil. For the production and publication of poems in America is immense. The situation resembles what the scouts saw ahead in The Territory: a living carpet of prairie that on approach became endless herds of bison, and from which clouds of birds swarmed up darkening the skies. Because the land is much richer than might have been expected, the temptation to spur forward, shooting without taking aim, is nearly irresistible. Yet as one follows the track that compilers of new poems have taken, one sees many feathers and bones strewn about, but too little, after all, to satisfy the seeker after poetry. If one is there to collect, the difficulties soon become clear.

In the first place, even before setting off on the trail of those who have recently gone before, absurd, desperate and unfair decisions must be made. An age limit, for example, has to be set: forty years for the new, the "younger" poets, leaving out of account the great, grizzled fellows who stand in plain view and ignoring those altogether solitary gray and hoary giants who are hardly remote even now in the Sixties. Our specimens are to be the young. At this the excitement of the venture diminishes, because it seems not often to have been the case during the past twenty years that the comers have made what is new in poetry; quite the opposite, the history of this art in the second third of the century is the product of the poets who are the stayers and who are continuing to make the future. (We ought not to be misled because we have been conditioned by the dazzling patterns of the American beauty industry and the built-in obsolescences required for the progress of our consumers' and militarists' technology: in art, change for change's sake makes nothing new necessarily.) But in anthology-making there are reasons for discriminating against our elders and betters, the simplest and strongest being economic—because recognized poets have their publishers, it is expensive to reproduce, though one may want to, such landmarks among the "younger" poets as, to name them at random, Roethke, Lowell, Jarrell, Schwartz, Kunitz, Berryman, Penn Warren, Wilbur, Shapiro, Eberhart, Cunningham, Nemerov. It is better to rule them out at the start anyway: the known need not be further explored, but cultivated.

In the second place, there is the difficult consideration of how many poets to exhibit and in what manner. Two ways of making an anthology come immediately to mind. The principle, apparently, of *The New American Poetry* was simply to present "the new poetry," its writers and ways. But because the idea was to adumbrate a movement, the result is a depressing sameness. On the other hand, the idea of the *New Poets of England & America* (editions 1,2) was to get lots of names across. In theory, these notions should do; in practice, the books produced frustrate the reader because their contents do not fully suggest the skill and range of many of their contributors. These horns of the anthological dilemma are good reason for despair. In consequence one daydreams of a benefactor who will give one a thousand pages to fill or a regular series of cheap paperbacks, or one projects a memorandum for Utopia in which is described a kind of Russian publishing institute that would provide the subsidy and vast readership for equally vast printings but function in the almost-free Western market. At any rate, I have here tried to solve the problem in a third way; since I have not intended showing the so-called "new poetry" exclusively, or the "new poets," again exclusively (these categories do not overlap in America!), I have had to regulate my choices in a way that may seem as arbitrary as the tactics taken in the other editorial tents. I have had to rely on my judgment of what is viable, credible work, a plan that I think was more difficult of execution because, truly, the country of contemporary poetry is a strange one. The wild mutants argue that the poems made by those deriving from old stocks are moribund, even extinct, mere feeble ghosts, while the old believers retort, reasonably, that the new variants must in the nature of the thing prove sterile. This opposed division is a problem in racial politics, so to speak; the poem-collector who takes it upon himself to judge between them now is foolishly bold: his purpose ought to be simply to bring them back, if not all happily together, at least all clearly enough alive. Nevertheless I am certain that the recent battles of the books of the Hip and the Square are already dismissible as merest fantasy.

Assuming one thinks one knows what is good when one finds it, does one, can one, know what he is looking for? To assert I have gone by what was once called taste or instinct would sound snobbishly atavistic to most readers. In any case, vocation or education, reputable words though they may still be, cannot suggest the resources upon which one draws in order to read or write new work today. For, in the creation and criticism of the arts, in our society, flair or intelligence or education refer to exactly what? As far as poetry is concerned, since around 1800, when not posing as Apollo or Satan, prophet, priest, bard or sybil or magician, telepath or psychopath, the poet has been regarded and has regarded himself (even in financial success) as at least a sort of *luftmensch*. But today he cannot even hope to live on air: there is too little available, and none of it fresh. We have nothing to go by any longer. We have nothing to go by, neither eyes nor ears nor mouths nor noses nor tongues. I am not sure whether brains or hearts or even hands are left us. Perhaps not even bowels. Many readers of poetry, and poets too, have not admitted this; or else they pretend to themselves and to each other, perhaps *must* pretend, that they are possessed of what were formerly believed vital human organs. Possibly blood, bone and muscle suffice to go on with, if going on is what is still wanted. Personally I think not, certainly not until new terms can be proposed.

My method in making this collection was as follows: when I was interested in a poet, I asked him to name pieces he liked from among those written over the last five years or so. Not everyone asked responded, allowing the inference that they didn't want to bother; not everyone who responded wished to be responsible for what was reprinted, or else wished to give me the responsibility, so that I felt free to sample as I pleased; again, not everyone I liked had enough exciting things to make his presence inevitable in the specimen anthology I had in mind; and finally, not everyone I wanted was priced low enough by his first publishers. Also, I discovered that among some of the poets in these pages who have been reprinted elsewhere, the best creations, to my mind, were often their longest. There are several things here, such as Henri Coulette's "War of the Secret Agents," that would probably never be reprinted intact elsewhere, yet which it seems most valuable to show in mutual juxtaposition. Not only are we not producing many excellent short poems, but the more intriguing young poets seem to be making towards something involving elements of the short story or the playlet, the confession of the diary, the scenario, or the Beckettesque monologue. Of course, my characterization can be promptly contradicted by one glance at the table of contents: W. S. Merwin, for example, who has published several volumes, is herein represented by new poems considerably briefer than his usual thing, and there are also Robert Creeley's very short poems. These latter seem to me, however, not selfcontained like Merwin's but the barely voiced or muttered bits of a much more complex and elusive history than the 'lyric' poem ordinarily accounts for. And, having determined to go somewhat farther with each poet than is the custom, so that he should be seen to advantage in a miscellany, it was necessary to restrict the number of contributors. Other editors excuse themselves for having omitted much good work for lack of space, but I must be pardoned for not including anything of many writers in whom I am greatly interested because, individually, they hadn't as many things as this book required. It was not my aim merely to bring out a collection of what I thought good poems: that task belongs to the editor who intends a yearbook, a project that should be undertaken by some publisher, by the way.

Aside from the fact that the poems collected here should in and of themselves reveal what I think is being done, the reader who knows the themes and shapes and modes of our older Twentieth-century poets (such as the "younger" poets named earlier), our immediate models and powers in the language, will see what their effects upon us have been. Apart, therefore, from the primary consideration of the *kinds* of poems one accepts as being current and vital, there remains a criterion which must be assumed fundamental, and yet resists being formulated. Whether or not I can say of a poem that, ultimately, I "like" it, I have tried to choose work which seems maturely wrought: powerful intellectually and potent linguistically, gifted with insight into itself, and solid, self-sufficient. More than this an anthologist cannot say for certain; and criticism, more accurately, fashions in criticism, he has to leave aside, more or less. Karl Shapiro, for example, has gone so far as to declare that the work of Eliot has perverted our sense of what poetry is or ought to be, and that a whole generation of study and derivation has resulted in what Harold Rosenberg describes as legions of university monks grinding poetry into dust in the dungeons of the academy; and W. D. Snodgrass echoes them in his irritation over recent Cantos, which have to be read according to a sort of ultrahighbrow flashcard technique of conditioned response to clues from everywhere and nowhere. The dissatisfaction of these critics (poets) is symptomatic of a shift in poetic climate and critical sensibility that is taking place. My own observation would be neutral: I would remark only that the influence of the poetry of Pound and Eliot, as well as of Williams, being as profound as it is, must be due not to any secret critical cabal according to the protocols of the Elders, but to the deeply felt power of their words and structures, whether superfastidiously obscure, falsely recondite, or utterly casual and colloquial.

In any case, the anthologist must try to avoid conformity like death itself. In putting the poems of this volume together I have never sought for social and artistic respectability or spiritual responsibility. Recently, mere rebellion, or disaffiliation, as it is oddly called, has been made into a standard; conversely, it is to be withstood by a kind of politely academic complexity or delicacy of indirection that seems to convey a mode of being or of perception that was still possible only yesterday. Art, that is, is the antidote to Rebellion, the proper way to distinguish among the crass imperatives of our American Way of Life. Both kinds of poems have their publishers, which may or may not be a sign of health. But both bore me because they are inherently conformist and respectable, for that is what a "position" that conforms to the poetic right or left or center must be—respectable. It is in fact astonishing that in our perfectly incredible world there should persist such old-fashioned camps. I should have thought poets belonged ahead, somewhere, somehow. The point about a camp is that poems belonging in it must be read according to a program: if you imitate certain drastic French poets, for example; or if you practice a kind of *collageisme* in which the scissors-and-paste work of the notebook have become the 'artifact'; or if you show you are refining and developing one of the 'discoveries' of Pound or Moore or Eliot or Williams, or even Whitman, in the same manner that the organic chemist hangs a dozen new substances from a certain poly-something ring (in the cant of manifesto-makers and their reviewers, this is termed "exploring the possibilities of"); if you resurrect Dada for a weekend or practice touch-typing on the endless towelpaper of neosurrealistic intuitional associationalism; if you count syllables only, or stick to couplets that have a certain Churchillian chime and moral gravity, or make iambic quatrains, or yawp out your syntactically weird prose with a combo, and so forth —then you are placeable, then you are acceptable in one of the camps or tents, not to call them movements, let alone schools. It would appear today an ineluctable requirement that a poem continue in or from the Romantic deliquescence of the past century, or else be crystallized according to the rule some personage in one of the many high places of the land has foredetermined (and the rules are not all by any means neoclassical only): each coven of addicts has its set little ritual for cooking-up, only more so. Apparently, for some the only "new poetry" acceptable is work too inchoate, too carelessly worded, made by careless people in uncaring moments according to half-baked theories about life and art, to be worth rereading, mere social, intellectual, even *emotional* "positions" expressed in adolescent or bookishly journalistic fashion, that is, rationalizations masquerading as poems—or else you must fall in with the "new poets," much too often backwardlooking, polite, secure, trite, dull. I have tried to obviate that dichotomy in this collection by choosing poems which are fully *formed*, and the book as a whole may suggest the enormous latitude I give to the word formed. The real trick to utterance, it seems to me, is to reveal something that, given our condition, is still somehow human, whether the guise in which it appears be old or new or "formally" null. And that which manages, given our conditions, to be human and alive is bound to be quite different from that which was human but is now dead. It is, I know, a most inexact standard, more like wishful-thinking made into a standard, whereas the living thing never measures up, or down, to a standard. But there it is. It is far too easy to reject, for example, Allen Ginsberg's "Kaddish" because it is a piece of work inconceivable under any familiar or accepted rubric. Rant, rot, rhetoric? Yes, all these. A poem? I think so, not only because it means to be a poem, but because it can be nothing else whatsoever; certainly it does not fail of poetry merely for failing to fit most of the templates. It is but one specimen of many I have picked up in the attempt to satisfy myself with works that put more questions about ourselves in our present circumstances than can be answered. And it is what I would call alive. It satisfies my hunger for something abstract enough to be poetry, and ahead of where we were yesterday, whenever yesterday was, in poetry. Of course what I may consider a dead poem will not seem such to its admirers; neither will the dead poet or critic or reader seem such to their friends. But I hope that what I think alive will at least seem that, whatever else it may seem in addition. I insist only that I believe most of us today find it very hard to know what is dead and what lives; perhaps, given our conditions we cannot know. The situation is so difficult, so very confused, that even Hemingway's obsession with what would or would not last seems a problem from a bygone and golden age when such a vain concern could be meaningful to the writer.

I suppose that finally the thing that seems most true to say about poetry today is that for both its writers and readers it may appear to be an incomprehensibly wasteful and notoriously futile luxury, as well as an absurd, often hideous, but sisyphean necessity. Those terms suit the conditions under which most of the work I believe in gets done. That so much is as good as I think it is, is almost miraculous.

Jascha Kessler

Los Angeles, California
February, 1963

American Poems

A CONTEMPORARY COLLECTION

James Wright

THE COLD DIVINITIES

I should have been delighted there to hear
The woman and the boy,
Singing along the shore together.
Lightly the shawl and shoulder of the sea
Upbore the plume and body of one gull
Dropping his lines.

Loping behind a stone too large for waves
To welter down like pumice without sound,
Laughing his languages awake, that boy
Flung to his mother, on a wrack of weeds,
Delicate words, a whisper like a spume
Fluting along the edges of the shore.

I should have been delighted that the cries
Of fishermen and gulls
Faded among the swells, to let me
Gather into the fine seines of my ears
The frail fins of their voices as they sang:
My wife and child.

Lovely the mother shook her hair, so long
And glittering in its darkness, as the moon
In the deep lily-heart of the hollowing swells
Flamed toward the cold caves of the evening sea:
And the fine living frieze of her Greek face;
The sea behind her, fading, and the sails.

I should have been delighted for the gaze,
The billowing of the girl,
The bodying skirt, the ribbons falling;
I should have run to gather in my arms
The mother and the child who seemed to live
Stronger than stone and wave.

But slowly twilight gathered up the skiffs
Into its long gray arms; and though the sea
Grew kind as possible to wrack-splayed birds;
And though the sea like woman vaguely wept;
She could not hide her clear enduring face,
Her cold divinities of death and change.

THE ACCUSATION

I kissed you in the dead of dark,
And no one knew, or wished to know,
You bore, across your face, a mark
From birth, those shattered years ago.
Now I can never keep in mind
The memory of your ugliness
At a clear moment. Now my blind
Fingers alone can read your face.

Often enough I had seen that slash
Of fire you quickly hid in shame;
You flung your scarf across the flesh,
And turned away, and said my name.
Thus I remember daylight and
The scar that made me pity you.
God damn them both, you understand.
Pity can scar love's face, I know.

I loved your face because your face
Was broken. When my hands were heavy,
You kissed me only in a darkness
To make me daydream you were lovely.
All the lovely emptiness
On earth is easy enough to find.
You had no right to turn your face
From me. Only the truth is kind.

I cannot dream of you by night.
I half-remember what you were.
And I remember the cold daylight,
And pity your disgusting scar

As any light-eyed fool could pity,
Who sees you walking down the street.
I lose your stark essential beauty,
I dream some face I read about.

If I were given a blind god's power
To turn your daylight on again,
I would not raise you smooth and pure:
I would bare to heaven your uncommon pain,
Your scar I had a right to hold,
To look on, for the pain was yours.
Now you are dead, and I grow old,
And the doves cackle out of doors,

And lovers, flicking on the lights,
Turn to behold each lovely other.
Let them remember fair delights.
How can I ever love another?
You had no right to banish me
From that scarred truth of wretchedness,
Your face, that I shall never see
Again, though I search every place.

AT THE SLACKENING OF THE TIDE

Today I saw a woman wrapped in rags
Leaping along the beach to curse the sea.
Her child lay floating in the oil, away
From oarlock, gunwale, and the blades of oars.
The skinny lifeguard, raging at the sky,
Vomited sea, and fainted on the sand.

The cold simplicity of evening falls
Dead on my mind,
And underneath the piles the water
Leaps up, leaps up, and sags down slowly, farther
Than seagulls disembodied in the drag
Of oil and foam.

Plucking among the oyster shells a man
Stares at the sea, that stretches on its side.
Now far along the beach, a hungry dog
Announces everything I knew before:
Obliterate naiads weeping underground,
Where Homer's tongue thickens with human howls.

I would do anything to drag myself
Out of this place:
Root up a seaweed from the water,
To stuff it in my mouth, or deafen me,
Free me from all the force of human speech;
Go drown, almost.

Warm in the pleasure of the dawn I came
To sing my song
And look for mollusks in the shallows,
The whorl and coil that pretty up the earth,
While far below us, flaring in the dark,
The stars go out.

What did I do to kill my time today,
After the woman ranted in the cold,
The mellow sea, the sound blown dark as wine?
After the lifeguard rose up from the waves
Like a sea-lizard with the scales washed off?
Sit there, admiring sunlight on a shell?

Abstract with terror of the shell, I stared
Over the waters where
God brooded for the living all one day.
Lonely for weeping, starved for a sound of mourning,
I bowed my head, and heard the sea far off
Washing its hands.

AT THE EXECUTED MURDERER'S GRAVE

(for J. L. D.)

> Why should we do this? What good is it to us? Above
> all, how can we do such a thing? How can it possibly
> be done?—FREUD

1

My name is James A. Wright, and I was born
Twenty-five miles from this infected grave,
In Martins Ferry, Ohio, where one slave
To Hazel-Atlas Glass became my father.
He tried to teach me kindness. I return
Only in memory now, aloof, unhurried,
To dead Ohio, where I might lie buried,
Had I not run away before my time.
Ohio caught George Doty. Clean as lime,
His skull rots empty here. Dying's the best
Of all the arts men learn in a dead place.
I walked here once. I made my loud display,
Leaning for language on a dead man's voice.
Now sick of lies, I turn to face the past.
I add my easy grievance to the rest:

2

Doty, if I confess I do not love you,
Will you let me alone? I burn for my own lies.
The nights electrocute my fugitive,
My mind. I run like the bewildered mad
At St. Clair Sanitarium, who lurk,
Arch and cunning, under the maple trees,
Pleased to be playing guilty after dark.
Staring to bed, they croon self-lullabies.
Doty, you make me sick. I am not dead.
I croon my tears at fifty cents per line.

3

Idiot, he demanded love from girls,
And murdered one. Also, he was a thief.
He left two women, and a ghost with child.

The hair, foul as a dog's upon his head,
Made such revolting Ohio animals
Fitter for vomit than a kind man's grief.
I waste no pity on the dead that stink,
And no love's lost between me and the crying
Drunks of Belaire, Ohio, where police
Kick at their kidneys till they die of drink.
Christ may restore them whole, for all of me.
Alive and dead, those giggling muckers who
Saddled my nightmares thirty years ago
Can do without my widely printed sighing
Over their pains with paid sincerity.
I do not pity the dead, I pity the dying.

4

I pity myself because a man is dead.
If Belmont County killed him, what of me?
His victims never loved him. Why should we?
And yet, nobody had to kill him either.
It does no good to woo the grass, to veil
The quicklime hole of a man's defeat and shame.
Nature-lovers are gone. To hell with them.
I kick the clods away, and speak my name.

5

This grave's gash festers. Maybe it will heal,
When all are caught with what they had to do
In fear of love, when every man stands still
By the last sea,
And the princes of the sea come down
To lay away their robes, to judge the earth
And its dead, and we dead stand undefended everywhere,
And my bodies—father and child and unskilled criminal—
Ridiculously kneel to bare my scars,
My sneaking crimes, to God's unpitying stars.

6

Staring politely, they will not mark my face
From any murderer's, buried in this place.
Why should they? We are nothing but a man.

7

Doty, the rapist and the murderer,
Sleeps in a ditch of fire, and cannot hear;
And where, in earth or hell's unholy peace,
Men's suicides will stop, God knows, not I.
Angels and pebbles mock me under trees.
Earth is a door I cannot even face.
Order be damned, I do not want to die,
Even to keep Belaire, Ohio, safe.
The hackles on my neck are fear, not grief.
(Open, dungeon! Open, roof of the ground!)
I hear the last sea in the Ohio grass,
Heaving a tide of gray disastrousness.
Wrinkles of winter ditch the rotted face
Of Doty, killer, imbecile, and thief:
Dirt of my flesh, defeated, underground.

A MESSAGE HIDDEN IN AN EMPTY WINE
BOTTLE THAT I THREW INTO A GULLEY OF
MAPLE TREES ONE NIGHT AT AN INDECENT
HOUR

Women are dancing around a fire
By a pond of creosote and waste water from the river
In the dank fog of Ohio.
They are dead.
I am alone here,
And I reach for the moon that dangles
Cold on a dark vine.
The unwashed shadows
Of blast furnaces from Moundsville, West Virginia,
Are sneaking across the pits of strip-mines
To steal grapes
In heaven.
Nobody else knows I am here.
All right.
Come out, come out, I am dying.
I am growing old.
An owl rises
From the cutter-bar
Of a hayrake.

TWO POEMS ABOUT PRESIDENT HARDING

ONE: *His Death*

In Marion, the honey-locust trees are falling.
Everybody in town remembers the white hair,
The campaign of a lost summer, the front porch
Open to the public, and the vaguely stunned smile
Of a lucky man.

"Neighbors, I want to be helpful," he said once.
Later, "You think I'm honest, don't you?"

I am drunk this evening in 1961,
In a jag for my countryman,
Who died of crabmeat on the way back from Alaska.
Everyone knows that joke.

How many honey locusts have fallen,
Pitched rootlong into the open graves of strip mines,
Since the First World War ended
And Wilson the gaunt deacon jogged sullenly
Into silence?
Tonight,
The cancerous ghosts of old con men
Shed their leaves.
For a proud man,
Lost between the turnpike near Cleveland
And the chiropractors' signs looming among dead mul-
    berry trees,
There is no place left to go
But home.

"Warren lacks mentality," one of his friends said.

Yet he was beautiful, he was the snowfall
Turned to white stallions standing still
Under dark elm trees.

He died in public. He claimed the secret right
To be ashamed.

TWO: *His Tomb in Ohio*

> ". . . he died of a busted gut."—(MENCKEN, on Bryan).

A hundred slag piles north of us,
At the mercy of the moon and rain,
He lies in his ridiculous
Tomb, our fellow citizen.
No, I have never seen that place,
Where many shadows of faceless thieves
Chuckle and stumble and embrace
On beer cans, stogies' butts, and graves.

One holiday, one rainy week
After the country fell apart,
Hoover and Coolidge came to speak
And snivel about his broken heart.
His grave, a huge absurdity,
Embarrassed cops and visitors.
Hoover and Coolidge crept away
By night, and women closed their doors.

Now junkmen call their children in
Before they catch their death of cold;
Young lovers let the moon begin
Its quick spring; and the day grows old;
The mean one-legger who rakes up leaves
Has chased the loafers out of the park;
Minnegan Leonard half-believes
In God, and the poolroom goes dark;

America goes on, goes on
Laughing, and Harding was a fool.
Even his big pretentious stone
Lays him bare to ridicule.
I know it. But don't look at me.
By God, I didn't start this mess.
Whatever moon and rain may be,
The hearts of men are merciless.

TWO HANGOVERS

NUMBER ONE

I slouch in bed.
Beyond the streaked trees of my window,
All groves are bare.
Locusts and poplars change to unmarried women
Sorting slate from anthracite
Between railroad ties:
The yellow-bearded winter of the depression
Is still alive somewhere, an old man
Counting his collection of bottle caps
In a tarpaper shack under the cold trees
Of my grave.

I still feel half drunk,
And all those old women beyond my window
Are hunching toward the graveyard.

Drunk, mumbling Hungarian,
The man staggers in,
And his big stupid face pitches
Into the stove.
For two hours I have been dreaming
Of green butterflies searching for diamonds
In coal seams;
And children chasing each other for a game
Through the hills of fresh graves.
But the sun has come home drunk from the sea,
And a sparrow outside
Sings of the Hanna Coal Co. and the dead moon.
The filaments of cold light bulbs tremble
In the music like delicate birds.
Ah, turn it off.

NUMBER TWO:
I try to waken and greet the world once again

In a pine tree,
A few yards away from my window sill,
A brilliant bluejay is springing up and down, up and down,
On a branch.

I laugh, as I see him abandon himself
To entire delight, for he knows as well as I do
That the branch will not break.

STAGES ON A JOURNEY WESTWARD

1

I began in Ohio.
I still dream of home.
Near Mansfield, enormous dobbins enter dark barns in
    autumn,
Where they can be lazy, where they can munch little ap-
    ples,
Or sleep long.
But by night now, in the bread lines my father
Prowls, I cannot find him: So far off,
1500 miles or so away, and yet
I can hardly sleep.
In a blue rag the old man limps to my bed,
Leading a blind horse
Of gentleness.
In 1932, grimy with machinery, he sang me
A lullaby of a goosegirl.
Outside the house, the slag heaps waited.

2

In western Minnesota, just now,
I slept again.
In my dream, I crouched over a fire.
The only human beings between me and the Pacific Ocean
Were old Indians, who wanted to kill me.
They squat and stare for hours into small fires
Far off in the mountains.
The blades of their hatchets are dirty with the grease
Of huge, silent buffaloes.

3

It is dawn.
I am shivering,
Even beneath a huge eiderdown.
I came in last night, drunk,
And left the oil stove cold.

I listen a long time, now, to the flurries.
Snow howls all around me, out of the abandoned prairies.
It sounds like the voices of bums and gamblers,
Rattling through the bare nineteenth-century whorehouses
In Nevada.

4

Defeated for re-election,
The half-educated sheriff of Mukilteo, Washington,
Has been drinking again.
He leads me up the cliff, tottering.
Both drunk, we stand among the graves.
Miners had paused here on the way up to Alaska.
Angry, they spaded their broken women's bodies
Into ditches of crab grass.
I lie down between tombstones.
At the bottom of the cliff
America is over and done with.
America,
Plunged into the dark furrows
Of the sea again.

A BLESSING

Just off the highway to Rochester, Minnesota,
Twilight bounds softly forth on the grass.
And the eyes of those two Indian ponies
Darken with kindness.
They have come gladly out of the willows
To welcome my friend and me.
We step over the barbed wire into the pasture
Where they have been grazing all day, alone.
They ripple tensely, they can hardly contain their
    happiness
That we have come.
They bow shyly as wet swans. They love each other.
There is no loneliness like theirs.
At home once more,
They begin munching the young tufts of spring in the
    darkness.
I would like to hold the slenderer one in my arms,

For she has walked over to me
And nuzzled my left hand.
She is black and white,
Her mane falls wild on her forehead,
And the light breeze moves me to caress her long ear
That is delicate as the skin over a girl's wrist.
Suddenly I realize
That if I stepped out of my body I would break
Into blossom.

Jane Cooper

OBLIGATIONS

Here where we are, wrapped in the afternoon
As in a chrysalis of silken light,
Our bodies kindly holding one another
Against the press of vision from outside,
Here where we clasp in a stubble field
Is all the safety either of us hopes for,
Stubbornly constructing walls of night
Out of the ordered energies of the sun.

With the same gratitude I feel the hot
Dazzle on my eyelids and your hand
Carefully opening my shaded breasts.
The air is very high and still. The buzz
And tickle of an insect glow and fuse
Into the flicker of a pulse. We rest
Closed in the golden shallows of a sound.
Once, opening my eyes, I betray your trust.

Startled, I break apart a shining blade
Of stubble as you bend to look at me.
What can your eyes lay claim to? What extreme
Unction after love is forced upon us?
The sun is setting now after its fullness,
While on the horizon like a fiery dream
Wakes the long war, and shared reality,
And death and all we came here to evade.

THE BUILDER OF HOUSES

for Sally Appleton

What was the blond child building
Down by the pond at near-dark
When the trees had lost their gilding
And the giant shadows stepped
To the water's edge, then stopped?
With intent fingers, doing a boy's work
In a boy's old sweater,
She hammered against her dear world's dirty weather.

Proud of her first house
Which boasted an orange-crate ceiling,
A pillow, a stuffed mouse,
And room for complete privacy
In the obvious crotch of a tree,
She skipped and swagged; rude cousins came stealing
With boys' laughter
And dismantled all but one branchy rafter.

She hunted almost till summer
Before her second find:
A post like a sunken swimmer
Deep in the marsh where ducks
Made nesting clucks and squawks.
With cautious tappings she fashioned a duck blind —
Or so her stepfather
Claimed when his autumn guns began to gather.

All winter in secret mourning
She toiled on her third house.
Three miles from the driveway turning
Up a forgotten path,
Risking her mother's wrath,
She tramped until her footprints filled with ice.
That bright glazing
Revealed one day her high and forbidden blazing.

In the very swaying top
Of a wind-swept sugar maple

She had built a bare prop—
Five boards to hold the crouch
Of a fugitive from search.
Here on this slippery and hard-won table
Armed with her hammer
She was tracked down by dogs' and parents' clamor.

There was only one more trial:
When frozen, brackish March
Gave way to floods in April
She rowed a sadly leaking
Scow, its oarlocks creaking,
Out to an island in the glittering reach,
And there, halfheartedly,
Began to floor the bend of a stunted tree.

Why was this last, secluded
And never-mentioned mansion
The one she never concluded?
Nor even the mellowing weather—
Routed her from her chosen foothold and passion;
This time house and view
Were hers, island and vision to wander through.

But less and less she balanced
Her boat on the sunrise water
Or from her window glanced
To where that outline glimmered;
Island and house were inner,
And perhaps existed only for love to scatter
Such long, carefully planned
And sovereign childhood with its unrelenting hand.

FOR THOMAS HARDY

(*in answer to* "Nobody Comes," *dated on my birthday*)

But you were wrong that desolate dusk
When up the street the crawl
Of age and night grew tall
As a shadow-self leaning away
From the gray religious husk
Of a streetlamp keeping watch above dead day.

You thought yourself alone
In a world whose nearest ghost
Was the alien pentecost
Of strumming telegraph, the throb
Of a motor quickly gone —
While over the animal sea my first-drawn sob
Straightened to share your dawn.

THE SUNDIAL

Take out of time that moment when you stood
On the far porch, a monolith of man,
And I raised one flag arm above my head:
Two statues crying out in stares of stone.

And take that moment when your flame-blue eyes
Blazed on me till true sunlight seemed to fail,
And all our landscape fell away like lies:
The burr of bees, grass, flowers, the slow sundial.

And take that moment after kneeling speech —
"Rare things must be respected," your lips said —
When moveless I withheld myself from reach;
Unmoving, gave my need to fill your need.

Behind us in the garden the great sundial
Began to stretch its shadow toward afternoon.
Nothing was altered. Only we sat still,
Spent with sane joy beyond the bees' numb drone.

THE FAITHFUL

Once you said joking slyly, "If I'm killed
I'll come to haunt your solemn bed,
I'll stand and glower at the head
And see if my place is empty still, or filled."

What was it woke me in the early darkness
Before the first bird's twittering? —
A shape dissolving and flittering
Unsteady as a flame in a drafty house.

It seemed a concentration of the dark burning
By the bedpost at my right hand,
While to my left that no man's land
Of sheet stretched palely as a false morning. . . .

All day I have been sick and restless. This evening
Curtained, with all the lights on,
I start up—only to sit down.
Why should I grieve after ten years of grieving?

What if last night I was the one who lay dead
While the dead burned beside me,
Trembling with passionate pity
At my blameless life and shaking its flamelike head?

W. D. Snodgrass

1

Child of my winter, born
When the new fallen soldiers froze
In Asia's steep ravines and fouled the snows,
When I was torn

By love I could not still,
By fear that silenced my cramped mind
To that cold war where, lost, I could not find
My peace in my will,

All those days we could keep
Your mind a landscape of new snow
Where the chilled tenant-farmer finds, below,
His fields asleep

In their smooth covering, white
As quilts to warm the resting bed
Of birth or pain, spotless as paper spread
For me to write,

And thinks: Here lies my land
Unmarked by agony, the lean foot
Of the weasel tracking, the thick trapper's **boot**;
And I have planned

My chances to restrain
The torments of demented summer or
Increase the deepening harvest here before
It snows again.

5

Winter again and it is snowing;
Although you are still three,
You are already growing
Strange to me.

You chatter about new playmates, sing
Strange songs; you do not know
Hey ding-a-ding-a-ding
Or where I go

Or when I sang for bedtime, *Fox*
Went out on a chilly night,
Before I went for walks
And did not write;

You never mind the squalls and storms
That are renewed long since;
Outside, the thick snow swarms
Into my prints

And swirls out by warehouses, sealed,
Dark cowbarns, huddled, still,
Beyond to the blank field,
The fox's hill

Where he backtracks and sees the paw,
Gnawed off, he cannot feel;
Conceded to the jaw
Of toothed, blue steel.

6

    Easter has come around
  again; the river is rising
    over the thawed ground
  and the banksides. When you come you bring
    an egg dyed lavender.
  We shout along our bank to hear
our voices returning from the hills to meet us.
  We need the landscape to repeat us.

    You lived on this bank first.
  While nine months filled your term, we knew
    how your lungs, immersed
  in the womb, miraculously grew
    their useless folds till
  the fierce, cold air rushed in to fill
them out like bushes thick with leaves. You took your
    hour,
  caught breath, and cried with your full lung power.

Over the stagnant bight
we see the hungry bank swallow
    flaunting his free flight
still; we sink in mud to follow
    the killdeer from the grass
that hides her nest. That March there was
rain; the rivers rose; you could hear killdeers flying
    all night over the mudflats crying.

You bring back how the red-
winged blackbird shrieked, slapping frail wings,
    diving at my head—
I saw where her tough nest, cradled, swings
    in tall reeds that must sway
with the winds blowing every way.
If you recall much, you recall this place. You still
    live nearby—on the opposite hill.

After the sharp windstorm
of July Fourth, all that summer
    through the gentle, warm
afternoons, we heard great chain saws chirr
    like iron locusts. Crews
of roughneck boys swarmed to cut loose
branches wrenched in the shattering wind, to hack free
    all the torn limbs that could sap the tree.

In the debris lay
starlings, dead. Near the park's birdrun
    we surprised one day
a proud, tan-spatted, buff-brown pigeon.
    In my hands she flapped so
fearfully that I let her go.
Her keeper came. And we helped snarl her in a net.
    You bring things I'd as soon forget.

You raise into my head
a Fall night that I came once more
    to sit on your bed;
sweat beads stood out on your arms and fore-
    head and you wheezed for breath,
for help, like some child caught beneath
its comfortable woolly blankets, drowning there.
    Your lungs caught and would not take the air.

Of all things, only we
have power to choose that we should die;
    nothing else is free
in this world to refuse it. Yet I,
    who say this, could not raise
myself from bed how many days
to the thieving world. Child, I have another wife,
    another child. We try to choose our life.

9

I get numb and go in
though the dry ground will not hold
    the few dry swirls of snow
and it must not be very cold.
A friend asks how you've been
        and I don't know

or see much right to ask.
Or what use it could be to know.
    In three months since you came
the leaves have fallen and the snow;
your pictures pinned above my desk
        seem much the same.

Somehow I come to find
myself upstairs in the third floor
    museum's halls,
walking to kill my time once more
among the enduring and resigned
        stuffed animals,

where, through a century's
caprice, displacement and
    known treachery between
its wars, they hear some old command
and in their peaceable kingdom freeze
        to this still scene,

Nature Morte. Here
by the door, its guardian,
    the patchwork dodo stands
where you and your stepsister ran
laughing and pointing. Here, last year,
        you pulled my hands

and had your first, worst quarrel,
so toys were put up on your shelves.
 Here in the first glass cage
the little bobcats arch themselves,
still practicing their snarl
  of constant rage.

 The bison, here, immense,
shoves at his calf, brow to brow,
 and looks it in the eye
to see what is it thinking now.
I forced you to obedience;
  I don't know why.

 Still the lean lioness
beyond them, on her jutting ledge
 of shale and desert shrub,
stands watching always at the edge,
stands hard and tanned and envious
  above her cub;

 with horns locked in tall heather,
two great Olympian Elk stand bound,
 fixed in their lasting hate
till hunger brings them both to ground.
Whom equal weakness binds together
  none shall separate.

 Yet separate in the ocean
of broken ice, the white bear reels
 beyond the leathery groups
of scattered, drab Arctic seals
arrested here in violent motion
  like Napoleon's troops.

 Our states have stood so long
At war, shaken with hate and dread,
 they are paralyzed at bay;
once we were out of reach, we said,
we would grow reasonable and strong.
  Some other day.

Like the cold men of Rome,
we have won costly fields to sow
   in salt, our only seed.
Nothing but injury will grow.
I write you only the bitter poems
    that you can't read.

   Onan who would not breed
a child to take his brother's bread
   and be his brother's birth,
rose up and left his lawful bed,
went out and spilled his seed
    in the cold earth.

   I stand by the unborn,
by putty-colored children curled
   in jars of alcohol,
that waken to no other world,
unchanging where no eye shall mourn.
    I see the caul

   that wrapped a kitten, dead.
I see the branching, doubled throat
   of a two-headed foal;
I see the hydrocephalic goat;
here is the curled and swollen head,
    there, the burst skull;

   skin of a limbless calf;
a horse's foetus, mummified;
   mounted and joined forever,
the Siamese twin dogs that ride
belly to belly, half and half,
    that none shall sever.

   I walk among the growths,
by gangrenous tissue, goitre, cysts,
   by fistulas and cancers,
where the malignancy man loathes
is held suspended and persists.
    And I don't know the answers.

The window's turning white.
The world moves like a diseased heart
   packed with ice and snow.
Three months now we have been apart
less than a mile. I cannot fight
    or let you go.

10

The vicious winter finally yields
   the green winter wheat;
the farmer, tired in the tired fields
   he dare not leave will eat.

Once more the runs come fresh; prevailing
   piglets, stout as jugs,
harry their old sow to the railing
   to ease her swollen dugs

and game colts trail the herded mares
   that circle the pasture courses;
our seasons bring us back once more
   like merry-go-round horses.

With crocus mouths, perennial hungers,
   into the park Spring comes;
we roast hot dogs on old coat hangers
   and feed the swan bread crumbs,

pay our respects to the peacocks, rabbits,
   and leathery Canada goose
who took, last Fall, our tame white habits
   and now will not turn loose.

In full regalia, the pheasant cocks
   march past their dubious hens;
the porcupine and the lean, red fox
   trot around bachelor pens

and the miniature painted train
   wails on its oval track:
you said, I'm going to Pennsylvania!
   and waved. And you've come back.

If I loved you, they said, I'd leave
   and find my own affairs.
Well, once again this April, we've
   come around to the bears;

punished and cared for, behind bars,
   the coons on bread and water
stretch thin black fingers after ours.
   And you are still my daughter.

LEAVING ITHACA

—to my plaster replica of the Aphrodite of Melos

Lady who stands on my long writing table,
I've brought seashells and fossils; I have put
Oak leaves weathered to gray lace at your feet,
Meaning I'll go your way when I am able.

Ten years now we've been transients since my mother
Mailed you, packed in towels, when I first married.
How often you've been boxed up, shipped or carried
From house to house, from one love to another.

When we first met, you'd lost a set of toes
And both your arms. Oh everloving Lady,
You had been ruined quite enough already;
Now the children have chipped off half your nose.

My first wife tried to keep you in the attic;
Some thought your breasts just so-so and your waist,
Thick with childbearing, not for modern taste.
My father thought you lewd and flicked your buttocks.

One giddy night, blonde Susan tipped your stand—
And you, true to your best style, lost your head.
You just won't learn how much smart girls will shed
This year. Well, we must both look secondhand.

Lady, we've cost each other. Still, it's been
Lovelier than I would have dared ask here:
My own house, my own woman, this whole year—
Lovelier than things will likely be again:

The handmade rough old farmhouse, out of sight
In overgrowth, in spruce and scrubby pines,
In lilac, in sumac, in the wild grape vines,
And arbor vitae on the lawn upright;

The tulips rising from forgotten beds,
Our welcome mat springing up green in clover,
Great maples scattering their winged seeds over
The chicken houses, the abandoned sheds

And the old barn, rotten, tremulous with owls,
The unpruned orchard, rank in its own mash,
Where pheasants nest, orioles fight and flash,
And evenings, silently, the groundhog prowls.

Now, of course, we have to move again
And leave the old house roughhewn as we found it,
The wild meadows and unworked fields around it—
No doubt it would have spoiled us to remain.

We'll leave our kittens, tagged for the new tenants;
The mother cat we couldn't bear to spay;
We'll take the dog along to give away
To someone who can pay for his dependents.

We'll leave the bunting and the scarlet tanagers
Here for the ladies' clubs, for our kind neighbors
Who know enough to get more from their labors,
Meet the right people or be better managers.

Already you can see them through the trees—
The bulldozed lots where men will pass their lives
In glossy houses kept by glossy wives
That have no past or future, but will please

The company. They go for the main chance
But always save the weekend for their passions;
They dress just far enough behind the fashions
And think right thoughts. They keep it in their pants.

Lady, we are going to have another child.
Was that the one thing you could send us, Lady?
You've brought us poverty enough already,
And *that* goes with us. Well, we are reconciled

Almost; almost. It's not smart, I suppose,
And where do we go now? We fume and worry;
We still just can't quite make ourselves feel sorry.
You've had these troubles; you know how it goes.

We'll try to live with evils that we choose,
Try not to envy someone else's vices,
But make the most of ours. We picked our crisis;
We'll lose the things we can afford to lose

And lug away what's left in orange crates:
Our driftwood, milkweed pods and Christmas cones,
A silver spoon Grandmother left, brook stones
Our daughters painted for my paperweights.

Snapshots, letters, the gimcracks that belong
To the children, the yellowing books we've read
For bedtime, and our own secondhand bed.
And you, Lady—we're taking you along.

MEMENTOS, ii.

I found them there today
in the third floor closet,
packed away
among our wedding gifts
under the thick deposit
of black coal dust that sifts
down with the months:
that long white satin gown
and the heavy lead-foil crown
that you wore once
when you were Queen of the May,
the goddess of our town.

That brilliant hour
you stood, exquisite, tall,
for the imperious Power
that drives and presses all
seed and the buried roots
to rise from the dead year.
I saw your hair,
the beauty that would fall
to the boy who won you. Today,
I wondered where,
in what dark, your wedding suit
lies packed away.

How proud I was to gain you!
No one could warn
me of the pride or of
the fear my love might stain you
that would turn your face to scorn —
of the fear you could not love
that would tease and whine and haunt you
till all that made me want you
would gall you like a crown
of flowering thorn.
My love hung like a gown
Of lead that pulled you down.

I saw you there once, later —
the hair and the eyes dull,
a grayness in the face —
a woman with a daughter
alone in the old place.
Yet the desire remains:
for the times when the right boys sought you;
to be courted, like a girl.
I thought of our years; thought you
had had enough of pain;
thought how much grief I'd brought you;
I wished you well again.

A FLAT ONE

Old Fritz, on this rotating bed
For seven wasted months you lay
Unfit to move, shrunken, gray,
No good to yourself or anyone
But to be babied—change and bathed and fed.
        At long last, that's all done.

Before each meal, twice every night,
We set pads on your bedsores, shut
Your catheter tube off, then brought
The second canvas-and-black-iron
Bedframe and clamped you in between them, tight,
        Scared, so we could turn

You over. We washed you, covered you,
Cut up each bite of meat you ate;
We watched your lean jaws masticate
As ravenously your useless food
As thieves at hard labor in their chains chew
        Or insects in the wood.

Such pious sacrifice to give
You all you could demand of pain;
Receive this haddock's body, slain
For you, old tyrant; take this blood
Of a tomato, shed that you might live.
        You had that costly food.

You seem to be all finished, so
We'll plug your old recalcitrant anus
And tie up your discouraged penis
In a great, snow-white bow of gauze.
We wrap you, pin you, and cart you down below,
        Below, below, because

Your credit has finally run out.
On our steel table, trussed and carved
You'll find this world's hardworking, starved
Teeth working in your precious skin.
The earth turns, in the end, by turn about
        And opens to take you in.

Seven months gone down the drain; thank God
That's through. Throw out the four-by-fours,
Swabsticks, the thick salve for bedsores,
Throw out the diaper pads and drug
Containers, pile the bedclothes in a wad,
And rinse the cider jug

Half filled with the last urine. Then
Empty out the cotton cans,
Autoclave the bowls and spit pans,
Unhook the pumps and all the red
Tubes—catheter, suction, oxygen;
Next, wash the empty bed.

—All this Dark Age machinery
On which we had tormented you
To life. Last, gather up the few
Belongings: snapshots, some odd bills,
Your mail, and half a pack of Luckies we
Won't light you after meals.

Old man, these seven months you've lain
Determined—not that you would live—
Just to not die. No one would give
You one chance you could ever wake
From that first night, much less go well again,
Much less go home and make

Your living; how could you hope to find
A place for yourself in all creation?—
Pain was your only occupation.
And pain that should content and will
A man to give it up, nerved you to grind
Your clenched teeth, breathing, till

Your skin broke down, your calves went flat,
And your legs lost all sensation. Still,
You took enough morphine to kill
A strong man. Finally, nitrogen
Mustard: you could last two months after that;
It would kill you then.

Even then you wouldn't quit.
Old soldier, yet you must have known
Inside the animal had grown
Sick of the world, made up its mind
To stop. Your mind ground on its separate
  Way, merciless and blind,

Into these last weeks when the breath
Would only come in fits and starts
That puffed out your sections like the parts
Of some enormous, damaged bug.
You waited, not for life, not for your death,
  Just for the deadening drug

That made your life seem bearable.
You still whispered you would not die.
Yet in the nights I heard you cry
Like a whipped child; in fierce old age
You whimpered, tears stood on your gun-metal
  Blue cheeks shaking with rage

And terror. So much pain would fill
Your room that when I left I'd pray
That if I came back the next day
I'd find you gone. You stayed for me—
Nailed to your own rapacious, stiff self-will.
  You've shook loose, finally.

They'd say this was a worthwhile job
Unlesss they tried it. It is mad
To throw our good lives after bad;
Waste time, drugs, and our minds, while strong
Men starve. How many young men did we rob
  To keep you hanging on?

I can't think we did *you* much good.
Well, when you died, none of us wept.
You killed for us, and so we kept
You; because we need to earn *our* pay.
No. We'd still have to help you try. We would
  Have killed for you today.

MANET: THE EXECUTION OF
EMPEROR MAXIMILIAN

Giving a gold coin to each soldier, he said, "Aim well, muchachos; aim right here," pointing to his heart. He waited with face turned upward, grave but calm.

Miramon and Jejias fell at once, but a second volley was required for the Emperor; he had wished to be shot in the body so that his mother might see his face.

Upon the Hill of Bells, the place of execution, the Austrian Empire erected a small but elegant chapel. The body, mutilated but fairly well preserved, was finally returned to Vienna where it received the full funereal honors of the Hapsburgs whose downfall was prefigured in his death.

These bunched soldiers, just now shooting the emperor,
  Stand with heels together, toes out, like ballet girls,
Though less tensely. In the main, we are made aware
  Of their white spats or white leather sabre-holsters.
They must suspect this is some notable affair
  Seeing their own parade uniforms and dress gear;
Yet one of them has shown up late—naturally—
  For this, the probable high point of his career,
And stands away to the one side, carefully
  Cocking his rifle. And yet he might be, perhaps—
Since his uniform seems a trifle less gaudy,
  With less braid but with a white band on a red hat—
An officer who's waiting to give the body
  The coup de grace. Meantime, all elegance and polish,
The men bend to their guns as if sighting some hard shot
  At the billiard tables; one they *might* accomplish,
Yet they would hardly be disgraced, if they should not.

In 1867, deserted by Napoleon III and the Pope, surrounded by intrigue and corruption, Maximilian assumed personal command of the remaining forces. On May 15, General Lopez (elsewhere erroneously called Gomez) betrayed Maximilian's headquarters at Queretaro for 20,-000 pesos. Once captured, Maximilian stead-

fastly rejected all schemes of Napoleon's agents
to spirit him away.

The peasants, peering up over the flat rock wall
    Which is the background, sprawl on their elbows or lay
Their heads on their crossed arms, like men who have gone
        dull
    In a tavern, or who must watch through a whole day
Of third-rate matadors practising on the farm.
    No doubt they were drawn by the marching and death
        drums,
The hope of gunflash or sight of the uniforms.
    How seldom anything splendid, decisive comes
Into their lives. And so they have kept their places
    For hours, logy as flies, out in the hot sun,
Knowing none of the names and none of the faces.
    Surely someone must tell them what it means, someone
Speak of nobility; proclaim that they are free.
    The daily quarrels and flirtatiousness go on.
Dusty as hollyhocks, their clustering faces are
    Vague as the rocks in the wall, from which they might be
An outgrowth—cool, distant, irrelevant as stars.

Having first naturalized the Swiss banker, Jecker,
so they might use Mexico's debts to him as a
pretext for intervention, the French staged a
fraudulent plebiscite to convince Maximilian he
had been overwhelmingly elected by the peons.
When Maximilian remained unconvinced, Napoleon threatened to offer the crown to some
other candidate.

Yet, for Maximilian, of whom all must agree
    He was intelligent, amiable, well-bred,
Generous even when one might scarce dare to be,
    Given to high ideals though frequently misled;
Whose face should show that firm nobility discerned
    Only in this bearded soldier of whom we know
Nothing; Maximilian for whom whole nations mourned;
    Two of whose generals decided not to go
Free, but died by him; whose wife, Carlotta, endured
    Sixty years mad with loss, hidden in a convent

Where though she lost her worst fears, she always referred
　　To her late husband as King of the Firmament;
Maximilian, who had dreamed that one day he might stand
　　At the top of some broad, magnificent staircase
And vouchsafe from that height of infinite command
　　One smile of infinite condescension and grace
On the human beings gathered around its base.

> Born July 6, 1832; son of the Archduke Franz
> Carl; brother of Franz Joseph I, Emperor of
> Austria. 1854, naval administrator; 1857, Viceroy
> of the Lombardo-Venetian Kingdom; 1864, Em-
> peror of Mexico.

Still, for Maximilian, for the man who stands here
　　In the midst of his own life—or to be exact,
Off to one side of his dying—he is nearly
　　Obscured by the smoke. Then, as a matter of fact,
Which of these figures is the man? Possibly this
　　Cool-eyed, white shirted one with the curled beard and
　　　hair
(Who might be an advisor). Or perhaps it is
　　The center one, since he's the only one who wears
A full coat; his face is older, lacks emotion;
　　Between the other two men, he holds both their hands.
But he's too pale; who would go to execution
　　Wearing a sombrero? This must be he who stands
Spread-legged, whose clenched free hand flaps up like a doll
　　While his face twists upward in a look that might be
Taken for great effort or for pain, as the balls
　　Break into his chest and, just at this instant, he,
Whoever he was, is now all finished being.

Robert Creeley

THE RHYME

There is the sign of
the flower—
to borrow the theme.

But what or where to recover
what is not love
too simply.

I saw her
and behind her there were
flowers, and behind them
nothing.

I KNOW A MAN

As I sd to my
friend, because I am
always talking,—John, I

sd, which was not his
name, the darkness sur-
rounds us, what

can we do against
it, or else, Shall we &
why not, buy a goddamn big car,

drive he sd, for
christ's sake, look
out where yr going.

THE DEATH OF VENUS

I dreamt her sensual proportions
had suffered sea-change,

that she was a porpoise, a
sea-beast rising lucid from the mist.

The sound of waves killed speech
but there were gestures —

of my own, it was to call her closer,
of hers, she snorted and filled her lungs with water,

then sank, to the bottom,
and looking down, clear it was, like crystal,

there I saw her.

A FORM OF ADAPTATION

My enemies came to get me,
among them a beautiful woman.

And — god, I thought, this will be the end of me,
because I have no resistance.

Taking their part against me even,
flattered that they were concerned,

I lay down before them and looked up soulfully,
thinking perhaps that might help.

And she bent over me to look at me then,
being a woman.

They are wise to send their strongest first, I thought.
And I kissed her.

And they watched her and both of us carefully,
not at all to be tricked.

But how account for love, even if you look for it?
I trusted it.

NAUGHTY BOY

When he brings home a whale,
she laughs and says, that's not for real.

And if he won the Irish sweepstakes,
she would say, where were you last night?

Where are you now, for that matter? Am
I always (she says) to be looking

at you? She says,
if I thought it would get any better I

would shoot you, you
nut, you. Then he pats her hair

into place, and waits
for Uncle Jim's deep-fired, all-fat, real gone

whale steaks.

A FORM OF WOMEN

I have come far enough
from where I was not before
to have seen the things
looking in at me through the open door

and have walked tonight
by myself
to see the moonlight
and see it as trees

and shapes more fearful
because I feared
what I did not know
but have wanted to know.

My face is my own, I thought.
But you have seen it
turn into a thousand years.
I watched you cry.

I could not touch you.
I wanted very much to
touch you
but could not.

If it is dark
when this is given to you,
have care for its content
when the moon shines.

My face is my own.
My hands are my own.
My mouth is my own
but I am not.

Moon, moon,
when you leave me alone
all the darkness is
an utter blackness,

a pit of fear,
a stench,
hands unreasonable
never to touch.

But I love you.
Do you love me.
What to say
when you see me.

OH NO

If you wander far enough
you will come to it
and when you get there
they will give you a place to sit

for yourself only, in a nice chair,
and all your friends will be there
with smiles on their faces
and they will likewise all have places.

A WICKER BASKET

Comes the time when it's later
and onto your table the headwaiter
puts the bill, and very soon after
rings out the sound of lively laughter—

Picking up change, hands like a walrus,
and a face like a barndoor's,
and a head without an apparent size,
nothing but two eyes—

So that's you, man,
or me. I make it as I can,
I pick up, I go
faster than they know—

Out the door, the street like a night,
any night, and no one in sight,
but then well, there she is,
old friend Liz—

And she opens the door of her cadillac,
I step in back,
and we're gone.
She turns me on—

There are very huge stars, man, in the sky,
and from somewhere very far off someone hands me
                                    a slice of apple pie,
with a gob of white, white ice cream on top of it,
and I eat it—

Slowly. And while certainly
they are laughing at me, and all around me is racket
of these cats not making it, I make it

in my wicker basket.

THE WIND

Whatever is to be come of me
becomes daily as the acquaintance
with facts is made less the point,
and firm feelings are reencountered.

This morning I drank coffee and orange juice,
waiting for the biscuits which never came.
It is my own failing
because I cannot make them.

Praise god in women.
Give thanks to love in homes.
Without them all men
would starve to the bone.

Mother was helpful but essentially mistaken.
It is the second half of the 20th century.
I screamed that endlessly,
hearing it back distorted.

Who comes?
The light footsteps
down the hall
betoken

—in all her loveliness,
in all her grimness,
in all her asking and staying silent,
all mothers or potentials thereof.

There is no hymn yet written
that could
provoke beyond the laughter I feel
an occasion for this song—

But as love is long-winded,
the moving wind
describes its moving colors
of sound and flight.

BALLAD OF THE DESPAIRING HUSBAND

My wife and I lived all alone,
contention was our only bone,
I fought with her, she fought with me,
and things went on right merrily.

But now I live here by myself
with hardly a damn thing on the shelf,
and pass my days with little cheer
since I have parted from my dear.

Oh come home soon, I write to her.
Go screw yourself, is her answer.
Now what is that, for Christian word?
I hope she feeds on dried goose turd.

But still I love her, yes I do.
I love her and the children too.
I only think it fit that she
should quickly come right back to me.

Ah no, she says, and she is tough,
and smacks me down with her rebuff.
Ah no, she says, I will not come
after the bloody things you've done.

Oh wife, oh wife—I tell you true,
I never loved no one but you.
I never will, it cannot be
another woman is for me.

That may be right, she will say then,
but as for me, there's other men.
And I will tell you I propose
to catch them firmly by the nose.

And I will wear what dresses I choose!
And I will dance, and what's to lose!
I'm free of you, you little prick,
and I'm the one can make it stick.

Was this the darling I did love?
Was this that mercy from above
did open violets in the spring—
and made my own worn self to sing?

She was. I know. And she is still,
and if I love her? then so I will.
And I will tell her, and tell her right . . .

Oh lovely lady, morning or evening or afternoon.
Oh lovely lady, eating with or without a spoon.
Oh most lovely lady, whether dressed or undressed or
                                    partly.
Oh most lovely lady, getting up or going to bed or sitting
                                    only.

Oh loveliest of ladies, than whom none is more fair,
                              more gracious, more beautiful.
Oh loveliest of ladies, whether you are just or unjust,
                              merciful, indifferent, or cruel.
Oh most loveliest of ladies, doing whatever,
                              seeing whatever, being whatever.
Oh most loveliest of ladies, in rain, in shine,
                              in any weather.

Oh lady, grant me time,
please, to finish my rhyme.

THE INVOICE

I once wrote a letter as follows:
dear Jim, I would like to borrow
200 dollars from you
to see me through.

I also wrote another: dearest M/
please come.
There is no one
here at all.

I got word today,
viz: hey
sport, how are you making it?
And, why don't you get with it.

THE END OF THE DAY

Oh who is
so cosy with
despair and
all, they will

not come,
rejuvenated, to
the last spectacle
of the day. Look!

the sun is
sinking, now
it's
gone. Night,

good and sweet
night, good
night, good, good
night, has come.

THE WIFE

I know two women
        and the one
is tangible substance,
        flesh and bone.

The other in my mind
        occurs.
She keeps her strict
        proportion there.

But how should I
        propose to live
with two such creatures
        in my bed —

or how shall he
        who has a wife
yield two to one
        and watch the other die.

Robert Mezey

THE FUNERAL HOME

In the environs of the funeral home
The smell of death was absent. All I knew
Were flowers rioting and odors blown
Tangible as a blossom into the face,
To be inhaled and hushed—and where they grew
Smothered the nostrils in the pungent grass.

Hyacinths of innocence, and yellow-hammers,
That beat the air at dawn, at dusk, to metal
Immortality, that flush where a bee clamors
For wine, are blooms of another color. See
How the flush fades as it descends the petal,
How deep the insect drinks, how quietly.

And curious, that among these ferns and rocks,
The violets flying a modest and blue elation,
And flapping ruffles of the white lilacs,
Shaking the air to tempt the golden bee,
Stiffen at the moment of consummation,
Swayed with guilt and weight of the bee's body.

These flowers, when cut and used, will remain ruddy,
As though made deathless in the very way
Their cutter kept the hue in the human body
That they were cut to celebrate and mourn.
The coffin has sprouted in dark mahogany
Out of them—edged, and shining like a thorn.

THE VISIT

The day she came, the trees and bushes slept
In cold content, lost in the snowy wind
That shook them with its changes, back and forth.
No bitten branch nor bare twig but was wrapt

47

In a thin membrane of transparent ice
Against the painful life of that white land,
Where living things bent to a final death
Or cunningly a deathless silence kept.
I rubbed my numb hands in a fireless house
And prayed for winter sleep with cloudy breath.
The oblique sun burned a black ring in my eyes;
Glare of the clear snow burned into my mind.

The lucky beasts who doze through such a season,
In hibernation till their rising day
And the renaissance that the new sun will make,
Were curled in humid caves, and with good reason.
Safely they snored and stirred in their warm tombs.
Some hardier fur, that braved the first frost, lay
Deep in the snow, and it would not awake;
A single bird descended, tired and freezing
In the wide naked sky, a single plume
Dropped from its dying body and forsook
What fell away into the falling gloom.
On such a day, she came to earth for me.

She fell through space, no heavier than air.
The darkness gathered round her, and her form
Dissolved and turned to darkness as she came.
On earth, she called her body back to her,
And wandered here, and here she saw me spent
And coming down with winter. Was she warm?
Against the cold she wore a cloth of flame,
Which only seemed too thin a dress to wear.
She dropped it to her feet, and somnolent,
Chilled with voluptuous fire, she said my name;
Her lips, half parted, murmured what she meant—
As darkness fell, I took her in my arms.

AGAINST SEASONS

Why should we praise them, or revere
The stations of the Zodiac,
When every unforgiving year
Drives us hence and calls us back?

The expectations we invent
Drift bodiless on the drifting air,
And who conceives them but must rent
The dark apartment of despair?

Days come and go, and we suppose
The future will bring something big;
But season after season throws
Rhomboids of sunlight on the rug.

They say a shattering horn will blow,
They say we must not be afraid,
But they are fools for saying so.
Endless meridians swing and fade,

All bodies in their orbits go,
The sky has nothing left to give.
We in this clash of circles know
Only the vicious ones we live.

Waiting for nothing, still, I wait,
Tired of God and of God's work.
Change is illusion—yet I hate
The silence and the changeless dark.

TO PHILIP LEVINE,
ON THE DAY OF ATONEMENT

Impenitent, we meet again,
As Gentile as your wife or mine,
And pour into affection's cup
Secular California wine.

Jewless in Gaza, we have come
Where worldly likenesses commence
And gather fury, but still keep
Some dark, essential difference.

Is it the large, unchiselled nose,
That monument to daily breath?
Is it some fiber in the heart,
That makes the heart believe in death?

God only knows. And who is he?
The cold comedian of our harm?
I wear its badge upon my sleeve,
You, like a scar on either arm —

But neither knows what good it does.
A voiceless darkness falls again
On this elaborate wilderness
And fills the empty minds of men

Where they sit drinking with their wives,
Children asleep, but not in bed,
Nothing to atone for but the cold
And blurred perspectives of the dead.

NO COUNTRY YOU REMEMBER

But for the steady wash of rain,
The house is quiet now. Outside,
Occasional cars move past the lawn
And leave the stillness purified.

I find myself in a dark chair
Idly picking a banjo, lost
In reveries of another time,
Thinking at what heavy cost

I came to this particular place,
This house in which I let my life
Play out its subterranean plot,
My Christian and enduring wife.

What if I paid for what I got?
Nothing can so exhaust the heart
As boredom and self-loathing do,
Which are the poisons of my art.

All day I resurrect the past.
This instrument I love so ill
Hammers and rings and, when I wish,
Lies in its coffin and is still.

I think of winter mornings when
Between bare woods and a wrecked shack
I came down deep, encrusted slopes,
A bag of dead birds at my back;

Then let my mind go blank and smile
At what small game the mind demands,
As dead time flickers in the blind
Articulation of my hands.

I know you must despise me, you
Who judge and measure everything
And live by little absolutes —
What would you like to hear me sing?

A strophe on the wasted life?
Some verses dealing with my fall?
Or would you care to contemplate
My contemplation of the wall?

I write from down here, where I live.
In the cold light of a dying day,
The covered page looks cold and dead.
And then, what more is there to say

Except, you read this in a dream.
I wrote nothing. I sat and ate
Some frozen dinner while I watched
The Late Show, and the Late Late.

AFTER HOURS

Not yet five, and the light
is going fast. Milky and veined
a thin frost covers the flooded
ruts of the driveway, the grass
bends to the winter night. Her face
is before me now; I see it

in the misted glass, the same
impenetrable smile, and I can feel
again on my bare shoulder
the dew of her breath. We made
a life in two years, a sky
and the very trees, lost in thought.

I know what it is, to be
alone, to have asked for everything
and to do without, to search
the mind for a face already dim,
to wait, and what it exacts.
I don't fear it, I say,

but I do, and this night
the wind against my window
and the top branches thrashing about
enter my life and I see
the coming time loose and dark
above me, with new strength.

YOU COULD SAY

Yesterday rain fell in torrents,
stripping the branches of leaves and
deepening the arroyo. Now,
although the sun glances like flint
at the edges of cars, houses,
antennas, the water remains.
It lies in the hollows of rocks
and in lakes on the roads. Last night
it signalled a great change; today
winter breathes at my window, and
a few last flies, stunned by cold
into fearlessness, nestle close
to my skin. Summer is burnt out.
Why does this season, with its joy
in killing and its hard iron breath,
always find me alone? You could say
but you won't and I am slowly
drifting away, I am growing
oblique like the sun, striking out
feebly at what is gone.

My love,
it was my nature to want you,
lascivious, aloof, a body
fresh as new-fallen snow, and as
cold. Like other men in my
desire, I asked for it and now
I have it — the wind, the black trees,
scum of ice on the roadside pools —
all that the rain promised, and more.

W. S. Merwin

ELEVEN POEMS

AIR

Naturally it is night.
Under the overturned lute with its
One string I am going my way
Which has a strange sound.

This way the dust, that way the dust.
I listen to both sides
But I keep right on.
I remember the leaves sitting in judgment
And then winter.

I remember the rain with its bundle of roads
The rain taking all its roads.
Nowhere.

Young as I am, old as I am,

I forget tomorrow, the blind man.
I forget the life among the buried windows.
The eyes in the curtains.
The wall
Growing through the immortelles.
I forget silence
The owner of the smile.

This must be what I wanted to be doing,
Walking at night between the two deserts,
Singing.

LOST MONTH

The light of the eyes in the house of the crow. Here the
gods' voices break and some will never sing again, but
some come closer and whisper. Never their names.

    There are no hinges. One side of the door is simply
forgotten in the other.

    The seven-branched permission appears already lit,
unasked, but the wind is the wind of parsimony, and
the shadows, which are numerous and large, strain at
their slender leashes. One fine day the first knives
come through the mirrors, like the fins of sharks.
The images heal, but imperfectly.

    We keep discovering parts of ourselves which came
to exist under this influential sign.

REUNION

At the foot of your dry well,
Old friend in ambush,
What did we expect?

Have we really changed?
You could never forgive me for
Pleasures divulged or defeats kept secret.

You have flowered in your little heat
Like an untrimmed wick.
It is plain that you are thinking

While I am thinking
How you have grown into your ugliness
Which at one time did not fit you.

Console your distaste for departures:
I find I brought only the one.
Hand me my coat.

Friend Reductio,
Would you have known delight
If it had knocked you down?

DESPAIR

Some lit theirs at both ends.
Some clutched theirs as a blind man does his cane.
Some sucked theirs like the only orange.
Some packed clean shirts and a few socks in theirs.
Some spent their lives looking for theirs and they
    were wearing it all the time.
Some neglected theirs but the roots found a way.
Some buried theirs. The stones tell when and where.

BY DAY AND BY NIGHT

Shadow, index of the sun,
Who knows him as you know him,
Who have never turned to look at him since the beginning?

In the court of his brilliance
You set up his absence like a camp.
And his fire only confirms you. And his death
    is your freedom.

IN THE GORGE

Lord of the bow,
Our jagged hands
Like the ends of a broken bridge
Grope for each other in silence
Over the loose water.
Have you left us nothing but your blindness?

SEPARATION

Your absence has gone through me
Like thread through a needle.
Everything I do is stitched with its color.

THE DEFEATED

Beyond surprise, my ribs start up from the ground.
After I had sunk, the waters went down.
The horizon I was making for runs through my eyes.
It has woven its simple nest among my bones.

NOAH'S RAVEN

Why should I have returned?
My knowledge would not fit into theirs.
I found untouched the desert of the unknown,
Big enough for my feet. It is my home.
It is always beyond them. The future
Splits the present with the echo of my voice.
Hoarse with fulfilment, I never made promises.

WITNESSES

Evening has brought its
Mouse and let it out on the floor,
On the wall, on the curtain, on
The clock. You with the gloves, in the doorway,
Who asked you to come and watch?

As the bats flower in the crevices
You and your brothers
Raise your knives to see by.
Surely the moon can find her way to the wells
Without you. And the streams
To their altars.

As for us, we enter your country
With our eyes closed.

FOREIGN SUMMER

Night goes, the fog lifts, there
Are the little fields
Drying like the laundry of strangers.
Foreign summer,
Even in your discarded costumes
I see now that your nakedness
Was never mine.

The day widens its revelation between us
Showing the roads
And I take up my empty hand
Which will be my torch this evening.

You yourself
Will go the way of everything I gave you.
You will notice the eyelids
Darkening on the ponds,
You will see the sightless streams of October,
You will pass by without recognition.

All up the road
The trees will miss you
When you have climbed their shadows.
Far from their embraces you will go on.
You will be happy.
Hope will have thought of you at every turn.
You will have the wrong key in your hand.

Henri Coulette

THE WAR OF THE SECRET AGENTS

I gave them bad habits and impossible loves.
I was arrogant,
heavy with ambition, sad.
They were footnotes with beautiful names;
they were passports without photos; they were dust,
and I took that dust in hand.

Dramatis personae

JANE ALABASTER	a scholar who is writing a history of the secret agents in France during World War II. She is concerned that many of them survive only under a cloud of treason. The lady is a spinster.
PROSPER	the chief of the secret agents in Paris; captured by Kieffer, he agrees to a deal whereby, surrendering his agents, he gains the promise from Kieffer of their safekeeping; he has a wife named NANCY.
ARCHAMBAULT	He is Prosper's radio operator, has red hair, very strange eyes, and writes bad poems. His Christian name (Gilbert) when pronounced in the French manner by Denise rimes with that of the following agent:
HILAIRE PENTECÔTE	who bears a most remarkable resemblance to a famous star of the French screen. Everything passes through his hands, as he is Air Movements Officer for the secret agents. He has no truck with doctors.
DENISE	Prosper's courier and Archambault's mistress, she has a sister, an identical twin named DESIRÉE, who, though not an agent, concerns herself to the point of obsession with their comings and goings.
CINEMA, PHONO	These two are among the surviving agents: Cinema the Mad, a rider on the Métro, who becomes a lighthouse keeper; big Phono, a Piccadilly Lazarus, who finds himself—in a tall glass.
BUCKMASTER	the London head of Special Operations Executive (or "the S.O.E." or "The Firm"), an organization consisting of such amateurs as Prosper. BODDINGTON is his second in command.

59

THE GERMANS   KIEFFER, the head of the Paris Gestapo, who
kept his promise as long as promises could
be kept; WULF, his second in command, who
ends as a mental patient; and YEAGER, a
member of the *Wehrmacht*.

THE OTHERS   MAMA BEE is a famous American medium
who tries to contact Prosper; MADAME GUÉPIN,
an ex-Resistance member; the ABBÉ OF ARDON,
a scholar; T. S. ELIOT, an editor.

I.   *Proem*

Prosper, Archambault, Gilbert, and Cinema —
romantic code-names
out of a teen-age novel
(*The Motor Boys and the Gestapo*).
Who can remain unmoved at the wedding
of youth and propaganda?

And so with their transmitters they came to France,
gifted amateurs
ready to die for England
and the S.O.E. How could they know
that what London told them was a nightmare
London had from Hollywood?

They will appeal to lovers of the absurd:
there they were, bulging
with codes and automatics.
Like debutantes slumming on Skid Row,
they couldn't be missed — they advertised,
and Death reads all the papers.

II.   *Jane Alabaster: A Letter to T. S. Eliot*

Dearest Possum,
                    It is as if I wrote you
not from this Paris,
the capitol of the Franks,
but from another, from a city
thrice more ancient, where gargoyles lean and leer
from parapets more subtle,

the ultimate prospect, the ultimate Paris.
The quest is over!
Now the last chapter: Gilbert
has promised to meet me—"to explain"
—as if explanation were still possible.
Now to confront him at last!

Do you realize I have spent some five years
with the words of ghosts,
in the company of men
who if they were not ghosts were more mad,
more broken than we imagine men can be
and still be men and not ghosts?

The quest is over, with what joy! what sadness!
Five years of my life
in order to crown my life—
well, surely, it was worth it, Possum.
Faber and Faber, you shall have your manuscript,
and I shall have my laurels—

and what laurels, too, for my text is human.
I have established
the reading of what moves,
breathes, and has known too much suffering.
Forgive me, dear friend, if I brag a little.
Tomorrow I am forty

and tomorrow in this ultimate Paris
I will meet Gilbert;
and meeting him, I will count
forty not as lonely women do
but as poets count their strophes, with a sense
of the timeless and the true.

III.   *Anonymous: On a Wall at Buchenwald*

11 November 1944—
I had one motive,
comfort, and I ended up
on a cold floor. I had one virtue,
loyalty, and I carried it far too far.
Goodbye, Goldilocks. Goodbye.

IV.   *Kieffer's Diary: 1942 - 5* [1]

1

It is like a musical composition
without music, pure
as music can never be,
or a monstrous, new form of blindfold
chess, where the moves are all Byzantine, unknown.
Am I mad from paper-work?

2

I find myself indifferent to places.
Paris means nothing;
Germany is forgotten.
I care only for the quirks of men.
Indeed, I study even the guards: brute Slavs,
dim Rumanian lackeys.

3

What a beautiful, evil son of a bitch
Gilbert proves himself!
Photostats of Prosper's
reports to London clutter my desk.
He writes with such style that my English improves.
Is there a style for pity?

4

I begin to know Prosper and his comrades.
There are even times
when I can sense their terror;
it is as though I were watching, too,
gazing up at my own office, at this light,
myself gazing at myself.

1. S. S. Sturmbannführer Hans Otto Kieffer
   counted beautiful
   women, good food, and sports cars
   among his passions, yet this diary,
   found after his execution, indicates
   a man of more than passion.

5

What was an amusement is now a danger.
Africa, Russia —
what I delayed must begin:
we will come in the night like bad dreams.
I look forward to meeting them, as I might
the authors of my childhood.

6

Name: Francis Suttill alias Prosper;
name: Gilbert Norman
alias Archambault; name:
Andrée Borrel alias Denise —
the shepherd has been introduced to his flock.
How shall I use my poor sheep?

7

A long talk with Prosper — I have given him
my formal promise:
no harm will come to his men,
none at all, if he cooperates.
He is as honest as a cavalryman;
London has sent me a child.

8

We two are caught up in a dream of pity.
We sit together
nodding over his reports,
his letters to his wife. Sleepwalker,
London was your God, and God has betrayed you.
You have my word, my pity.

9

He consents!

10

                We have bagged over a thousand.
They are in the net,
and not one drop of blood spilt.
What a beautiful, evil Gilbert —
to have given me so many charming birds,
to have given me their songs!

11

A little treatise on the uses of song,
on the radio game?
London responds arming us.
Yes, yes, they are sending us arms,
and I am sending messages to their wives.
Dear God, the uses of song!

12

London has sent us a Major Boddington,
whom we wined and dined
and sent back in ignorance;
four commandoes whom we had to kill.
So blood has been spilt, so I must ask myself,
How can we lose? and still lose.

13

Wulf and I have been trying to burn records;
there are too many.
And my lost sheep, where are they?
Exhausted beyond caring, we laugh,
hearing the festival of guns in the street,
in the Bois de Boulogne.

14

They say I am to be hanged. I don't know why.
The four commandoes?
No, it is that they fear me,
that they fear what I don't know I know.
They fear what I might say, yet I would not speak:
the methods . . . the methods go on. . . .

v. *Witnesses: On the Backs of Envelopes*

1   Major Boddington

Truth, madam, is a waif in the wilderness —
it dies of neglect.
We have chosen to forget,
deliberately, out of kindness.
Truth is, Archambault was the English Judas
we have chosen to forget.

2   Colonel Yeager

The retreat from Paris was an Olympics
for half-mad cripples.
We limped and raved across France,
the great jaw of chaos at our heels.
Germany had no time for Kieffer's promise;
she was preparing to die.

3   Madame Guépin

Denise in the prison at Fresnes told me,
— —*Gilbert me protège.*
She told me this, yes, and this,
— —*C'est Gilbert qui nous a tout vendus.*
The dead are dead, and we live out the new lies,
without love, beyond betrayal.

VI.   *The Abbé of Ardon: A Page from an Official History*

Her sister, hearing of her imprisonment,
confronted the *Boche*
and begged to be made captive,
though innocent of Denise's crime.
Whatever their motive, they complied.
The Lord have mercy on her.

They came finally to the Natzweiler Camp,
where the sick were gassed;
and her sister being ill,
Denise begged to be chosen as well.
Thus, these daughters of France came to embrace Death.
The Lord have mercy on them.

VII.   *Cinema, at the Lighthouse*

I admire the driven, those who rise from choice
as from a sick bed.
I was of that company,
as you are, as he is whom you seek.
What little I know you must know, or have guessed.
Prosper, I assume, is dead;

we last met beside the train that had brought us
into Germany.
We came upon each other
in the steam of the brakes, and his eyes
were those of a blindman or a cuckold. We passed
each other without speaking.

The other one I met once on an airfield
my first night in France.
If I remember rightly,
we did not speak; perhaps we nodded;
perhaps his hand touched my elbow. I recall
only the scent of the cut hay

and the overwhelming sensual delight
I knew momently
under the dangerous moon.
Your prey was of the breathing darkness
wherein, without father, Cinema was born —
he was midwife at that birth.

A ghost of a cockney with a gift of tongues,
what did I become?
Whatever Cinema did,
and he did it well. And when I slept,
I could hear the nations underneath my ear,
and my dreams were of pure light.

This has the ring of nonsense about it, no?
How can I tell you?
How can I explain to one
never there? I was a courier
and rode the Métro, disguised differently
everyday. I was no one,

I was what I seemed, I did not have to think.
This house is the grave
of Cinema, and this light
his epitaph. How can I explain
the dead? The dead are an extravagant cheese,
nor have the sad gift of tongues.

VIII.   *Mama Bee: The Séance*

The right frame of mind, honey, is a calm hope,
what Daddy Bee calls
"a gentle expectancy."
It's the practical approach to faith.
Now, my guide's a little Spanish spirit named
Guadalupe—you'll like her.

Let's begin . . . Guadelupe, Guadalupe,
can you hear me, dear?
Guadalupe, can you hear?
Am I getting through to you, honey?
We are trying to contact Major Suttill,
Major Francis Suttill, dear.

—¿Como esta, Mama? ¿Que pasa? ¿Subtle who?
—No, Guadalupe,
it's Major Francis Suttill;
we think he passed over in the war.
Do you know him, honey, in the Great Beyond?
Honey, do you know him there?

(I am here. I wear the mufti of a shade.)
Is he there, honey?
Am I getting through to you?
(Mufti, and memory like a chain . . .)
Guadalupe, Guadalupe, are you there?
—Vaya con Dios, Mama.

IX.   *Denise: A Letter Never Sent*

Desirée,
          I find it most bitter that you,
my sister, my twin,
should set your heart against me.
Gilbert is my love, my protection;
I am no streetwalker in a scarlet sheath
tripping through the Place Pigalle.

How stupid, how petite-bourgeoise to unleash
such rabid, convent-
bred imaginings upon
me—your own sister, your twin!
I had thought to share the sweetness of my love.
How carefully I chose words!

I wanted so to tell you of this strange gift,
for I must conceive
of love as something given—
I wanted to tell you of Gilbert,
of how he crams my very being with such joy,
and of his marvelous eyes.

Now you have come between me and my mirror.
How can I behold
my image—yes, our image
—without rancor? I must school myself
to be an only child, beyond reflection,
marvelous to his marvelous eyes.

x.   *Archambault: A Suspicious Poem*

The lost addresses of the soul are these:
the great estate
with mermaids at the gate
or the cold-water flat with wolves—
wherever loneliness like a disease
or a wildflower evolves—

or where like alabaster in the dark
she lies in wait
whom you would celebrate
in the exclusion of the mind,
whom you, in dreams, inchoate, known as ark,
crucible, and rind—

or where, powerful, irresponsible,
you turn away
from what the others say,
and—like a mirror come to life—
make of duplicity the single rule,
and use it like a knife.

XI. *Orphan Annie: The Broken Code*

8 - 9 - 12 - 1 - 9 - 18 - 5 - 16 - 5
14 - 20 - 5
3 - 15 - 20 - 5 - 9
19 - 1 - 4 - 15 - 21
2 - 12 - 5 - 1 - 7 - 5 - 14 - 20 - 6
15 - 18 - 11 . . .

XII. *Phono, at the Boar's Head*

Thanks, I will.
               You understand he wasn't mad?
even in the end?
Oh, I was there, I saw him,
I saw his mind become more lucid,
hour by hour, thought by thought, lucid as the flesh
of the old, the very old,

a Chinese wisdom. I give you the Chinese.
I give you nothing
you can't find out for yourself,
except the last look of Archambault:
the delicate, livid face of a red-head,
with one brown eye, and one blue.

We knew at Mauthausen that we were to die.
My fear kept me sane;
I talked to it in my head.
Show these bastards how to die, I said.
My days were like dreams in which I dreamt my death.
I lived like a coward.

And all the while Archambault lay there smiling
like a god damn saint.
There is nothing left to lose,
he said. *Nothing but my frigging life,*
I said, but he didn't hear me, or he heard
and knew there was nothing left.

Did you know, he laughed, *they captured us in bed,*
in Denise's bed?
I woke up with their torches
in my face. I dreamed they would be there,
and they were, and I wasn't afraid. I sighed,
I think, with satisfaction.

I rose. I stood stock still. I read the letter-
ing on the light bulb.
I saw Denise's nipples,
taut, purple, oddly oval. I heard
the embarrassed creaking of the German coats.
I smelled the oil on their guns.

I saw the world, and I gave back what I saw.
I was a mirror,
nothing more. I was faithful;
I gave an eye for an eye. Can they
execute a mirror? There will be gunfire
and an end to reflection.

—*Show these Gothic bastards how to die,* I said.
—*You show them,* he said,
and don't forget to say "cheese."
—*Fuck your brown eye, and your blue,* I said,
and in the morning the guards took him outside
and shot him, and I waited,

knowing I would be next, saying, *Show them how* . . .
I waited nine months,
and the Americans came.
It was 80 days before I walked.
I was Lazarus come to Piccadilly,
unseeing among strangers,

among the accusing Buckmasters of London,
among the whispers
of *treason, treason.* —*Bad show,*
a bad show best forgotten, old man,
Buckmaster said. He was embarrassed for me;
I had neglected to die.

It's madness, I know, but they wanted us dead.
Are the files neater
if you die? What Prosper did
when he dickered with that German crank
was to save a few lives —oh, not the best lives,
but a few; that was his crime.

And when you ask me why I drink, I must say
I don't know. Is it
in memory of Prosper,
of silly Prosper? Do I follow
Archambault by fifths, a brown eye, and a blue?
The Buckmasters of this world —

do I drink to stomach them? Or the coward
who waited nine months
and the Americans came?
Well, I give you the Americans.
Now one more for the road, and do count your change;
the publican is a cheat.

XIII. *Buckmaster on the* BBC

The rose is more than a handful of petals;
the hive is greater
than the meandering bee.
We are moved by, and toward, absolutes:
the rose for meaning, and the hive for purpose.
The rose, the hive, and Special

Operations Executive —or "the Firm,"
as we called it then —
what do they have in common?
Well, what is bravery without a cause?
How could any one of us fall asleep nights
without the rose and the hive?

XIV. *Wulf, at the Asylum*

The doctors regard me as a classic case,
and that's the story
that I've doctored up for them,

or you, or any who come rooting
among my hems and haws. I'm a specialist;
I prescribe what you ask for,

and you ask for Kieffer. How will you have him?
wriggling on a rope?
or alone, the middle-aged
dandy, mooning over a desk lamp?
Kieffer, you know, could never cross his ankles
for fear of spoiling his shine:

we Germans have been seduced by our tailors.
We move, when we march,
in an ecstasy of tabs
and ribbons—the beautiful soldiers! [2]
So Kieffer sat there at his great cherry desk,
his ankles never touching;

behind him, on the wall, framing his heavy,
military head,
the yellow map of Paris,
the tacks glistening like caught insects.
Gilbert stood among the shadows in the office,
and the shadows were like dark

angels landing and taking off. They whispered,
Gilbert and Kieffer,
or was it the sound of wings?
Desirée had turned against Denise,
as sisters turn against sisters in a world
carnivorous, but Kieffer

would delay, admiring his boots, and the tacks
glistened all night long.
Desirée was so lovely,
I could not believe she had a twin,
that that dark hair, those lost eyes, that crooked mouth
had any equals ever.

2.   It must be noted that the speaker was not
        himself a soldier,
        for he belonged, like Kieffer,
        his superior, to the Gestapo,
        though that organization was properly
        known as the *Sicherheitsdienst*.

So Desirée came to Kieffer now and then,
and Kieffer would smile,
as a parent smiles, hearing
a good lesson, and send her away.
This all happened a long time ago, and we
have all died, this way or that.

xv.   *Prosper: A Letter to Nancy* [3]

Le Sacré-Coeur trembles on the window pane,
a lorry rumbles
down the street, a baby cries
somewhere below stairs —who was it said,
Paris is for Englishmen and pickpockets —
lovers go to the country?

I am having one of my headaches today.
In a few minutes
the others will start arriving:
lumbering Phono, mad Cinema,
and the star-crossed lovers, of course. I must play
the greybeard for these children.

Their reports, as usual, will be worthless.
The Jerry troop train
is late. It is! It isn't!
But no, it was already arrived.
And then the arguments will start. Cinema
will storm out. Denise will cry.

3.   Nancy Suttill has remarried. Her husband
is a car salesman
in Leeds. They have two children,
a daughter and an adopted son;
the son has been named Prosper, Prosper
Pulkinghorn, to be exact.

It is Nancy Pulkinghorn who has observed
that this strange letter
may be the work of Kieffer
(see Section Eleven of Part Four).
At this late date, she is unable to say
more than this on this matter.

When my cigarettes are gone, and my patience,
why, then they will leave,
and I will peer down at them,
there, on the street, and I will whisper,
God damn you, God damn you, I'm through, I've had it,
I'm going home to Nancy!

Then, I'll look around the room and see the flowers
Denise has brought me
for my desk. I'll arrange them,
giving them water, knowing I'll stay.
It is the thought of you that keeps me going,
but this is the way I go.

XVI.   *Hilaire Pentecôte, His Horoscope*

They were at a corner table in the Ritz.
Jean Gabin, she thought.
He looks just like Jean Gabin.
Hilaire had removed his dark glasses,
and his grey eyes were both wary and amused.
"You are Gilbert," she stated.

"No, I was Gilbert. I am Hilaire Pentecôte.
They are but two names
among many. There are names
on every side, waiting to be used.
I help myself. But what is it that you want?"
"You are Gilbert," she answered.

"I want justice. I confront you with your past."
"Ah, my dear lady,
you want justice in the Ritz?"
He made a soft gesture, and his hand
described the four-star luxury of the room.
"There were two of you," she said.

"The English Gilbert and the French Gilbert.
You are the latter,
the one of whom Denise said,
'C'est Gilbert qui nous a tout vendus.'
You sold them out, and a dead man got the blame."
"You are absolutely right,"

he said. "But what of it? what is it to you?"
"Just this," she answered,
"it wasn't Gilbert Norman,
and it wasn't that poor demented
girl, Desirée, either. My book will clear them."
"And label me a traitor?"

"Yes." "No," he answered, "that isn't possible."
"But it is. I can . . ."
"No," and he smiled; "no, you can't,
for I'm not the traitor that you think."
"But they gave the papers to you for the planes,
and you gave them to Kieffer,

and Kieffer copied them, and gave them back . . ."
She was breathless now,
frightened by the innocence
that rode upon his smile. "Yes," he said,
"but I did only what London told me to —
I was London's instrument.

There was an underground beneath the underground.
They protected it.
Kieffer never guessed the truth;
he was too busy counting the sheep
London let him have by way of sacrifice —
fifteen hundred little lambs!"

"No," she murmured, but she knew he spoke the truth.
It was as if truth
had an odor about it,
distinct, acrid as a camphor lamp.
"How do I know," she asked, "that you are not telling
me an enormous lie?"

"You don't," he answered, and then he laughed.
                                    "Do you think

London will confirm
what I whisper in the Ritz?
No, but you can prove me innocent.
Write your book, and see if London prosecutes:
London will not lift a hand."

"Dear God," she said, "it is all too horrible:
fifteen hundred lives!"
"Yes," he said, and touched her hand.
"It was no business for angels,
or sheep, or an Ivanhoe like our Prosper.
I am a religious man,

and it grieves me." He said this almost shyly.
She looked at Hilaire.
"You have then a religion?"
"Yes," he said. "May I ask what it is?"
"Christian Science," he answered in a fine confusion.
"I am interested myself,"

she said, "in astrology. May I ask you
your chronology?
I have an ephemeris
in my bag." She took it from her purse.
"September 2, 1909,
at eleven in the night."

As he sipped his drink, a black currant syrup,
she drew a rough chart
on the back of the wine list.
"Your horoscope," she said, "is under
the dominance of an almost exactly
rising Neptune, and Neptune

implies a taste for adventure—on all planes,
and in all senses,
embracing on the one hand
an aspiration toward the mystical,
and on the other, the mundane, a penchant
toward secret activities,

with a liability toward duplicity.
I beg your pardon,
but it's here your drama lies,
especially as your planet's caught up
in a most spectacular grand-cross,
and a grand-cross, my dear sir,

demands a working out in terms of violence."
He clutched the wine list
to him. "Now that," he said, "that
is fascinating. I mean really."
She smiled and nodded, and they sat silently
till the waiter brought the check.

,xvii.   *Epilogue: Author to Reader*

Reader, we are getting ready to pull out.
Archambault has packed
the transmitter in an old
suitcase. Denise is combing her hair.
We are meeting Phono and Cinema downtown
in a second-rate bistro.

Prosper has been worrying about Phono;
he has a bad cough.
—And Cinema, I worry
about Cinema, who must insist
on a trenchcoat, of all things. But life goes on,
even here, in its own way.

Reader, you have been as patient as an agent
waiting at midnight
outside a deserted house
in a cold rain. You will ask yourself,
What does it all mean? What purpose does it serve,
my being here in this rain?

Reader (you will be known henceforth by that name),
there is no meaning
or purpose; only the codes.
So think of us, of Prosper, silly
Prosper, of Archambault of the marvelous eyes,
of Denise combing her hair.

Philip Levine

SMALL GAME

In borrowed boots which don't fit
and an old olive greatcoat
I hunt the corn-fed rabbit,
game fowl, squirrel, starved bob cat,
anything small. I bring down
young deer wandered from the doe's
gaze, and reload, and move on
leaving flesh to inform crows.

At dusk they seem to suspect
me, burrowed in a corn field
verging their stream. The unpecked
stalks call them. Nervous, they yield
to what they must: hunger, thirst,
habit. Closer and closer
comes the scratching which at first
sounds like sheaves clicked together.

I know them better than they
themselves, so I win. At night
the darkness is against me.
I can't see enough to sight
my weapon, which becomes freight
to be endured or at best
a crutch to ease swollen feet
that demand but don't get rest

unless I invade your barn,
which I do. Under my dark
coat, monstrous and vague, I turn
down your lane, float through the yard,
and roost. Or so I appear
to you who call me spirit
or devil, though I'm neither.
What's more, under all, I'm white

and soft, more like yourself than
you ever would have guessed before
you claimed your barn with shot gun,
torch, and hounds. Why am I here?
What do I want? Who am I?
You demand from the blank mask
which amuses the dogs. Leave me!
I do your work so why ask.

GANGRENE

Vous *êtes sorti sain et sauf des basses* calomnies,
vous *avez conquis les coeurs.*   ZOLA, *J'accuse*

One was kicked in the stomach
until he vomited, then
        made to put back
into his mouth what they had
brought forth; when he tried to drown
        in his own stew
he was recovered. "You are
worse than a nigger or Jew,"

the helmeted one said. "You
are an intellectual.
        I hate your brown
skin; it makes me sick." The tall
intense one, his penis wired,
        was shocked out of
his senses in three seconds.
Wakened, he watched them install

another battery in
the crude electric device.
        The genitals
of a third were beaten with
a short wooden ruler: "Reach
        for your black balls.
I'll show you how to make love."
When two of the beaten passed

in the hall they did not know
each other. "His face had turned
        into a wound:
the nose was gone, the eyes ground
so far back into the face
        they too seemed gone,
the lips, puffed pieces of cracked
blood." None of them was asked

anything. The clerks, the police,
the booted ones, seemed content
        to inflict pain,
to make, they said, each instant
memorable and exquisite,
        reform the brain
through the senses. "Kiss my boot
and learn the taste of French shit."

Reader, does the heart demand
that you bend to the live wound
        as you would bend
to the familiar body
of your beloved, to kiss
        the green flower
which blooms always from the ground
human and ripe with terror,

to face with love what we have
made of hatred? We must live
        with what we are,
you say, it is enough. I
taste death. I am among you
        and I accuse
you where, secretly thrilled by
the circus of excrement,

you study my strophes or
yawn into the evening air,
        tired, not amused.
Remember what you have said
when from your pacific dream
        you awaken
at last, deafened by the scream
of your own stench. You are dead.

PASSING OUT

The doctor fingers my bruise.
"Magnificent," he says, "black
at the edges and purple
cored." Seated, he spies for clues,
gingerly probing the slack
flesh, while I, standing, fazed, pull

for air, losing the battle.
Faced by his aged diploma,
the heavy head of the X-
ray, and the iron saddle,
I grow lonely. He finds my
secrets common and my sex

neither objectionable
nor lovely, though he is on
the hunt for significance.
The shelved cutlery twinkles
behind glass, and I am on
the way out, "an instance

of the succumbed through extreme
fantasy." He is alarmed
at last, and would raise me, but
I am floorward in a dream
of lowered trousers, unarmed
and weakly fighting to shut

the window of my drawers.
There are others in the room,
voices of women above
white oxfords; and the old floor,
the friendly linoleum,
departs. I whisper, "my love,"

and am safe, tabled, sniffing
spirits of ammonia
in the land of my fellows.
"Open house!" my openings
sing: pores, nose, anus let go
their charges, a shameless flow

into the outer world;
and the ceiling, equipped with
intelligence, surveys my
produce. The doctor is thrilled
by my display, for he is half
the slave of necessity;

I, enormous in my need,
justify his sciences.
"We have alternatives," he
says: "Removal . . ." (And my blood
whitens as on their dull trays
the tubes dance. I must study

the dark bellows of the gas
machine, the painless maker.)
". . . and learning to live with it."
Oh, but I am learning fast
to live with any pain, ache,
growth to keep myself intact;

and in imagination
I hug my bruise like an old
Pooh Bear, already attuned
to its moods. "Oh, my dark one,
tell of the coming of cold
and of Kings, ancient and ruined."

SIERRA KID

"I've been where it hurts." The Kid

He becomes Sierra Kid

Sheep shit and fever gold
Fouled the lower hills.
I passed Slimgullion, Morgan Mine,
Campo Seco, and the rotting Lode.
Dark walls of sugar pine—,
And where I left the road

I left myself behind;
  Talked to no one, thought
Of nothing. When my luck ran out
Lived on berries, nuts, bleached grass.
    Driven by the wind
    Through great Sonora Pass,

    I found an Indian's teeth;
    Turned and climbed again
Without direction, compass, path,
Without a way of coming down,
    Until I stopped somewhere
    And gave the place a name.

    I called the forest mine;
    Whatever I could hear
I took to be a voice: a man
Was something I would never hear.
    Whatever lived in me
    Softened and was free.

He faces his second winter in the Sierra

A hard brown bug, maybe a beetle,
Packing a ball of sparrow shit—
    What shall I call it?
Shit beetle? Why's it pushing here
At this great height in the thin air
    With its ridiculous waddle

Up the hard side of Hard Luck Hill?
And the furred thing that frightened me—
    Bobcat, coyote, wild dog—
Flat eyes in winter bush, stiff tail,
Holding his ground, a rotted log.
    Grass snakes that wouldn't die,

And night hawks hanging on the rim
Of what was mine. I know them now;
    They have absorbed a mind
Which must endure the freezing snow
They endure and, freezing, find
    A clear sustaining stream.

He learns to lose

She was afraid
Of everything,
The little Digger girl.
Pah Utes had killed
Her older brother
Who may have been her lover
The way she cried
Over his ring—

The heavy brass
On the heavy hand.
She worried it for weeks
Clenched in her fist
As if it might
Keep out the loneliness
Or the plain fact
That he was gone.

When the first snows
Began to fall
She stopped her crying, picked
Berries, sweet grass,
Mended her clothes
And sewed a patchwork shawl.
We slept together
But did not speak.

It may have been
The Pah Utes took
Her off, perhaps her kin.
I came back
To find her gone
With half the winter left
To face alone—
The slow grey dark

Moving along
The dark tipped grass
Between the numbed pines.
Night after night
For four long months
My face to her dark face
We two had lain
Till the first light.

Civilization comes to Sierra Kid

They levelled Tater Hill
    And I was sick.
First sun, and the chain saws
    Coming on; blue haze,
        Dull blue exhaust
Rising, dust rising, and the smell.

Moving from their thatched huts
    The crazed wood rats
By the thousand; grouse, spotted quail
    Abandoning the hills
        For the sparse trail
On which, exposed, I also packed.

Six weeks. I went back down
    Through my own woods
Afraid of what I knew they'd done.
    There, there, an A & P,
        And not a tree
For miles, and mammoth hills of goods.

Fat men in uniforms,
    Young men in aprons
With one face shouting, "He is mad!"
    I answered: "I am Lincoln,
        Aaron Burr,
The aging son of Appleseed.

"I am American
    And I am cold."
But not a one would hear me out.
    Oh God, what have I seen
        That was not sold!
They shot an old man in the gut.

Mad, dying, Sierra Kid enters the capital

What have I changed?
I unwound burdocks from my hair
    And scalded stains
        Of the black grape
And hid beneath long underwear
    The yellowed tape.

Who will they find
In the dark woods of the dark mind
Now I have gone
Into the world?
Across the blazing civic lawn
A shadow's hurled

And I must follow.
Something slides beneath my vest
Like melted tallow,
Thick but thin,
Burning where it comes to rest
On what was skin.

Who will they find?
A man with no eyes in his head?
Or just a mind
Calm and alone?
Or just a mouth, silent, dead,
The lips half gone?

Will they presume
That someone once was half alive
And that the air
Was massive where
The sickening pyracanthus thrive
Staining his tomb?

I came to touch
The great heart of a dying state.
Here is the wound!
It makes no sound.
All that we learn we learn too late,
And it's not much.

Irving Feldman

The good girls are down from the Bronx
Wearing ceramic jewels like a badge,
Whirling peasants skirts as they dance.
And the straighthaired blondes who busted college
Are carrying Proust around with Lawrence.
As I knew them.

And the lost girls float with dark eye
And pale face, their diction studied, voices firm,
Like Cassandras crying, I will not cry!
The thin young girls have matronly arms,
And here and there walks a beauty.
As I knew them

And the Stalinists are there with guitars
And argyle socks, plaid shirts on their swelling chests,
Flogging the strings for the czar of czars,
The people; meanwhile their girlfriends' breasts
Are like brave new worlds, and simple as the stars.
As I knew them

Cooler than you, man, or I, the hipsters are cool
As the shining mountain stream at dawn
That trickles to its hidden crystal pool
Where the lapwing drinks, the hare, the fawn;
So cool are the hipsters, cooler, more cool.
As I knew them

The long white ones the sun has never seen,
Their eyes are like the earthsweated coal
Behind their sunglasses' evergreen,
Picking picking up the soul
With cocaine, heroin, and benzedrine.
As I knew them

87

Making it making it on manna are the shades,
Digging strange gods in the marijuana;
Today they're corn-fed Buddhas or de Sades,
Tomorrow Gnostics in the same old Nirvana;
Angular and drowsy in a world they've never made.
As I knew them

And the Bus. Ad. boys are down with their dates,
Callow faces poised like cream above their coffees.
The law students have mouths like revolving gates,
On their adam's apples, dazzling bowties
Gallop through blizzards of polka-dots.
As I knew them

And the fairies are out, dressed as queens
And princes; wads of cotton candy
Their little behinds in their tight blue jeans,
Like a terrible lollipop the head of one dandy.
And many are neo-Augustinians.
As I knew them

And the dykes are policing the johns,
They're cut in half by heavy belts, their necks
Are like clubs; but the voices of their minions
Are weak and strangled in their stomachs;
And small unshaven men are running their errands.
As I knew them

And the hoods with violet truncated faces
Like frost-bitten potatoes, and the lean
And crew-cut professional satyrs,
One with an Austrian voice like vaseline
Asking, 'Und vere are the Graces?'
As I knew them

The bald bachelors of forty are out, as always,
They go to bed with the morning papers,
Where all our lives are a little play;
Their weekend *Times* on cafeteria tables
Spreading its fatal wings over Sunday.
As I knew them

And the bums leak in from the Bowery
Like tiny black dust no sieve can catch.
Old Italians are silent in doorways,
They just happen to live here, and they scratch.
But the Olympians never come down from their parties.
As I knew them

Creep on, creeps! On Greenwich, on MacDougal,
Brothers, sisters, children mine!
So monstrous and so innocent all,
Because so young, and getting younger all the time.
—The Grace of Heaven is games in Hell.
As I knew them

In that glorious night our lives, my love,
Were like a marquee's blinking lights,
Blinking on and off. And did we ever move!
Seeming to dance out words all night,
Hand in hand now you now I going on and off.

1.   THE ARK

Ghetto-born, depression-bred,
Squeezed between the finger and thumb
Of Famine and traditional Dread,
I learned all history's a pogrom.

Scared tutelage of the dead.
The hand that strokes the silken shawl,
I learned, may not strike red.
A Jew's defense, the Wailing Wall.

Learned to be patient under blows,
Suspect the world, yet ready to be
Wiped across my neighbor's nose,
Chided then for being filthy.

Learned the cost of life in cents,
To measure every ring and rag.
Saw Israel's shining tents
Fold up like a doctor's bag.

Learned the little-bourgeois ruse;
To save the day against the night,
And night for day, then lose
Them both, worrying if I were right.

Free of the flood, our ghetto tied
Smugly to the rope of His wrath,
We thought to put the word aside
Like the dirty ring after a bath.

*

The fog in curtains under the lamps,
Kitchen vapors on the pane,
Smoke puffing out with cramps,
Distant gossip in the drain.

Furniture that I recall:
Solemn lumbar embassy,
Plump and bowing from the wall
To whisper, Comfort's ecstasy.

Sleep! those lotus-eaters said,
A conspiracy in the bowels restores
The interlocking trust of bread.
Sleep alone never bores.

A liver lounging in a pot;
Mama boiling the kitchen runes.
Always I see her face a blot
In the sacred oval of the spoons.

Grey and sweet and shining eyes,
Freckled arms that took with ardor
The scalds and bundles of sacrifice
—To fill again love's larder.

She kneeled to dust the furniture,
But rose with an abstracted eye.
What was it she had seen there?
In spite of all, people die.

In spite of every daily care,
The wash, the rent, sickness, meals,
The building of a life is air,
For death is something else.

The pot grew cool by afternoon
And wore a smiling beard of tears.
A drop crawled drowsily down,
And fell, like the falling years.

The radiator knocked like a ghost,
Outside, the wind and bawling cats.
My father nodded at his post,
Messiah thundered fireside chats.

Papa—shy, sour, slow—
Enduring the worried years like a stone,
Falling, falling asleep over the radio,
Dreaming of his son.

That all proclaimed the quotidian,
And should the day ache with glory,
Prescribed a little medicine.
Grandeurs of our infirmity.

Fed up with the narrow pot,
Every day I ate disgust.
Dishes, death, closet of rot,
Who invented this can of dust!

Well, I flew away from all that—
The old rock, the old ark
Hung aloft on Ararat—
Crow lost in a world of wrack.

2.   WRACK

A lonely music arose and bid
Me follow. And I went.
Under the night's unwaking lid
I learned what dying meant.

And took upon me mourner's weed
And ashes of a fallen son,
Thinking Esau's desert seed
Was happier than my own,

And being choked with memory
I might thereby blot out my name,
Thought breath came best in beggary.
Alas! it was all the same.

With orphan girls I slept it off,
My patrimony of dust.
Hammered down the nights like a cough:
Ghetto contempt, ghetto distrust.

Wintered, paltry, threadbare things,
I took their nakedness to wrap
My fatted calf — Jacob of strings
And straw, curtains of blue burlap.

Ah, those tenement pastorals,
Dressed in the rags of love and such,
Shepherding little animals
Who asked for nothing needing too much.

*

Her sweat, mascara, breasts implied
The wherewithal to float an affair,
And to her poverty testified
A certain lankness, pallor of hair.

At dawn her eyes opened wide,
Like doors on an empty hall, the stair,
The street's cold light — till I was outside,
And doubting I had been there.

*

Along the street a winter wind
Rattled its elementary war.
Breathless armies arrived and grinned,
Entered their trench by a subway door.
Leaflets from trees proclaimed the end.
And the wind came on as before.

THE HAND

1

Aboard a train three thousand miles
From whatever home I might call mine
I saw, across a valley of mortar and tiles,
The setting sun on a thousand windows shine
Till they were flames that woke and tossed
Like the thousand torches of a host
That marched in glory on the hill.
They marched, not I, I confess,
Stupid and dull with hopelessness.
Round and tart as an apple the wind fell,
The weather pursed and smelled of fall.

Then I remembered this was the day
When wine is lit in our feeble clay
And all who move find moving is to pray,
Who touch the world but touch in play.
For then the Torah is unwound, rewound,
To the fiddle's sound and foot's sound,
Rewound from that triumphant end,
Blest vision of the promised land,
Back to the bitter start
Where Creation cracks apart,
And then again begun.
But for this minute history's undone
And man is free, though through the long year
Week by week he give sweat and prayer
And never glimpse the promised shape.
Then, prophets riot in the grape,
And kings go dancing in the law,
Husbands leap, wives bring straw,
And greybeards stamp their feet for sign
As though to press the world to wine.
I, who was a child, would carry then
A tiny paper flag among the men,
A living apple crowned its wooden staff
And there a candle flared to laugh
Aloud the drunken mystery of night,
And made that dangerous glory a game
Where all that was not wine was flame.

I never knew, consumed in the ritual of light,
What the apple or the candle meant.

. . . So long ago, forgot when I went
Away. Nothing to mourn or repent;
Not lost, nor happy either.
The sun went down, the host under the hill.
And whether those symbols held a sweeter
Secret I was ignorant still.

2

Now must I in darkness turn,
Search for key and grope the latch
This umber hour of fall; and watch
The bats, and hear owls in the barren
Trees mourn. What curse has fallen? —
That I must sit in darkness sullen
Hour on hour by this stupid table
Counting down the minutes' babble
And cannot move, no, not for a match!
Was this the payment of my days?
I raised this hand to strike my flesh
— And saw it suddenly ablaze!
I say my hand was light
Which all the blackened room made light.
The darkness was a sea of wine
Burning burning up the brine
Till the moment where I stood was bare,
And Canaan rising there.

'All that is not this burning hand,
Let it stand as wax may stand,
Run down or turn to smoke,
Be burning wine that it may raise
Up joy and hope in endless praise,
Though they be more to burn.
Let flame arise in the year's urn
Till all that dying is a brand,
Let fire on Canaan come, let it run
Laughing through the promised land
Till beginning and end are one,
Bound together on the fiery vine,
This burning evil, the other death.'

I moved this hand of mine,
I breathed, and this truth burned up my breath.

ASSIMILATION

I dreamt the other night I was in Heaven,
That I rose up like a sundae with leaven.
I was there in the Old Folks Home playing pinochle
     and checkers
And up above us is a picture of Old Abe who fried
     the neggers.
Everything is free and grade-A. Then I turn over
     my card.
It says, 'What's good for Ford is good for God.'
And all the boys are gathered sitting around
     the Televidge,
Clear as day you can see God's own image.
He talks sweet and low and he looks like Ed Murrow,
The music's by Gilbert and Ed Sullivan; then it all
     goes blurro.
And Maxie whispers, 'He's Self-Sponsored,
     Self-Applauded, Self-Rated,
One and Almighty. It's a quality show and never
     outdated.'
'Haha,' I say, 'boy, that's rich!'
'Shhh,' says Bennie, 'He owns half of Miami Bich!
But I figure I'll unload 'cause the market looks
     too bullish.
But Barney whispers, 'Don't do nothing fullish!'
So I hang on and buy till the ticker goes screwy
And I'm 10 million bucks ahead and the bears are
     all blooey.
The sky's full of stars going around in their tracks
     like at Graumans Chinese,
And they start handing out autographed menus from
     Lindys,
The guys're all drunk and there are B-girls and bagels
And free silver dollars straight from Las Vegals
And Bella grabbed me and said, 'Hey, we're all angels!'
But I'm worried, why does Mr. Mortie have to run after
     the models?

Can't he stick to his dressmaker's dummy and keep out of
    the Catskills?
That buyer from Phillie! That union contract! O, I wanna
    scream, Halp!
Seventh Avenue's waiting for my scalp.
But Gimbels takes a thousand and Macys takes ten
    and then it's bam!
And I buy Rausye a mink for her old persian lamb.
And Grossingers was giving a banquet at Woolwoits
And Sollie was laughing it up trying on the skoits,
And Albie said, 'Moishie's under the Boardwalk
    gettin' laid.'
And Sadie said, 'Come on, let's go sit in the shade.'
And Marvin sank a heaver and Joey hooked from the side,
Then Creepie drove in for a lay-up while the other guys
    cried.
And Bernie pulled a mouse-trap and Skinnie's pass hit
    the mark,
And forever and ever the Mighty Babe stood swattling 'em
    outta the park.
Then after the spelling-bee we have a map-drawing contest
Of the United States and teacher says mine's the best.
But Sidney and me, we snuck into the Loews
And this guy sits down and starts tickling our knees.
And I say, 'Leave us alone, mister,' and he says,
    'Say please.'
And then he says, 'Wanna see the scar under my kiltie?'
And I look and o my god it's uncle Miltie!
And they all think the Lone Ranger is really a crook,
And on the street papa says hello to Mr. Bashook.
Then the kids all pile in and we start throwing rocks.
On the radio Uncle Moe says, 'Irving, there's a present
    in the icebox.'
O god, I feel all soft and I wanna cry and twitch.
There's a card, it says, 'For your throat, a thirty-year
    itch.'
And there's a can the size of a man, and mama's in it!
'Mama,' I cry, 'I found you again!' 'Don't talk,' says she,
    'itt!'
And I'm standing in my crib and I say, 'Papa, buy me a
    tri-cycle.'
And he spreads his wings and smiles like the American
    Ikele.

And it's always dark and everything's free and you never
  hear No.
But I can't breathe and think I'll drown in the stuff
  and nobody'll know.
And I wake up kicking and screaming, Lemme go!
  Lemme go!

THE LOST LANGUAGE

I have eaten all my words,
And still I am not satisfied!
Fourteen thousand and twenty blackbirds
Hushed under my side.

And when I think of what I have written
Or might have and can and shall write
—My life, this appetite,
But how shall I eat the food forgotten?
And think of how my envy like a lust
Kept me up all night with its tease,
And how the night unveiled a noble bust
When I thought of glory—but that doesn't please.
So much ambition,
And so little nutrition.

Après le déluge, moi.
There it is, all the sad tale—
A perfect post-diluvian male,
And other humanist ta ran ta ra.
For, after all, it's only disgrace,
At the very best, to outlive
(Half-monadnock, half-sieve)
The saddest thing in the life of the race.

And when I think how many fathoms deep
Debris of that mighty birth . . .
O then there were words in the earth!
That were the things they named
And lay like manna in easy reach,
And when you spoke, there was speech

Very hungry and not a little ashamed,
For passion is no longer food,
I have taken up again,
In ghostly parody, pot and pen,
And sit to gnaw my chattering brood.

One cup of Lethe and it's always too late.
Where are you, *o liebe breyt?* *

* Yiddish for 'bread.'

John Logan

A Verse Re-telling

1   The terrible wrath I say
     Bore to Greece
     Every kind of sorrow
     And sent to hell the souls
     Of fighting men leaving them
     Food for birds and dogs
     Through some will of the Gods
     Who brought Achilles and the King
     Together over the matter at
     First of the Priest's daughter.

2   The Priest came to the beached
     Ships of the Greeks
     With prize of gold and the powerful
     Staff of the God Apollo
     Who sends or holds off evil;
     He prayed for the luck of Greece
     At war with Troy so long,
     For a fast return home,
     And asked in his stead his daughter's
     Freedom from the King's bed.

3   But this King of Men
     Does not send
     Her free: she will grow old
     He said a long way
     She will grow old a long
     Way from her own country
     And she shall work her loom
     And share my bed; now get
     The hell out the King said
     And you will keep your skin.

4   The old Priest's heart
    Shook as he left
    And walked without a word
    Or sound alone along
    The shores of the moaning sea
    ('Oh Son of Leto hear me!)
    God of the bright bow
    If I have burnt you thighs
    Of bull and goat now let me weep
    Your arrows for my tears!

5   Within their quiver silver
    Arrows clanged
    At the radiant God's side:
    He shot from the holy height
    With speed of night and knelt
    By ships and rang his silver
    Bow; its terrible song
    Struck the busy dog
    And mules and men, and again many
    Fires burned the dead.

6   The arms of the goddess turn
    Themselves as white
    Smokes of sacrifice
    That rise for Greece until
    Achilles calls the well
    To council, and the seer
    Whose gifts have kept the swift
    Fleets tells all the guilt
    Of overlord and King; now hate
    Turns itself toward him:

7   The King's face flares —
    You hound of hell
    When have you told the good
    Or given any aid
    But bad or loved any
    But your own god damned
    Word: you know well
    How much I want the girl;
    If I give her up to end this death
    What shall I have instead?

8   Achilles rose shouting
Most glorious King
Most greedy of men indeed
What shall the lusty Greeks
Give for prize; can you find
A common store of wealth
Out of our pillaged towns?
Give her up and wait; when God
Lets the walls of Troy fall
You shall be triple paid.

9   Achilles you have guts
And you may be
Godly, but here's a wit
You'll find hard to beat.
Do you expect to keep
A girl while I sit and wait?
No you don't! I'll take
Your prize or Aias' or bear
The prize of Odysseus away—for someone
This will be a hard day.

10   Achilles said you wise
Son of a bitch
Whose war is this anyway?
Those mountain shadows and sounds
Of the sea for a long time
Put Troy from me: no Trojan
Spears and men have robbed
Sheep or corn or wives
In lands of mine, and today I could lead
My beaked ships away.

11   Walk out then said the King—
Others honor me;
Take your rage and your men.
Play cock-of-the-walk with them!
I'm sick of your taste for blood
Anyway and your touted bravery
Is some affect of the gods—
You don't scare me and you won't
Forget my strength when it has sent
Your girl weeping from your tent.

12   Achilles trembled and said someday in your
      Despair remember what I now swear:
      By this staff your men shall reel to the Trojan
      God, shall feel his eyes that flame and glint
      Along his gold mask to guide his lance
      He flings from his glorious arm bringing heavy
      Death and the melancholy clang of brass;
      He slays from life in his shining limbs as lean
      And stripped as the holy staff of Zeus I cut from the
          hill.
      And by these things shall Kings tell Achilles!

13   As for me I no more
      Obey the King.
      He may take the girl
      He gave; of all else
      Beside my good black ship
      Not a thing, or mark, his dark
      Blood will soon be flowing
      Down this idled spear.
      Achilles and his King now end
      Their war of hate full saying.

14   The King puts a fast
      Ship to sea—
      The daughter of the Priest and twenty
      Oarsmen under Odysseus
      Captain: her white sail
      Swells, the gray god whis-
      pers busily by the stem;
      Others bathe them in the salt
      And unspoiled sea and twist their prayers
      With curls of sacrifice.

15   The horns of the sun-cattle gleam
      Along the hill
      As Apollo's Priest and daughter
      Weep together by the well-
      built altar and the King's
      Men rinse their hands
      To scatter holy grain
      Beautiful as morning
      Rain and catch the blood of bulls
      And flay their quivering hides

16   And wrap the bits of thigh
     In fat the Priest
     Shall flame with wine above the hiss
     Of prayers, while at the fire's
     Edge they plunge their bronzed
     Forks and eat the brilliant
     Inner parts that hold the God.
     At last they feast, and shift
     The mixing bowls of wines and sing
     Loud to the Archer King.

17   The Priest's daughter home
     Achilles' prize
     Gone he sat alone
     By the gray seas sat
     Alone by the black ships
     And wept, lifting his arms:
     This fastest runner this shortest
     Lived Achilles cried
     As a child to its mother, eating his heart
     For the lost fury of the fight.

                              After Homer Iliad 1
                       and after a terracotta figure
                          of an Etruscan warrior

HONOLULU AND BACK

To James Brunot

Ruth had been moved out of her job in an
Hawaiian school for leaving it on Good
Friday to go to church. It was tough to
Get the place for her, but the year the war
Was through you couldn't ship without a job.
Ruth was pregnant and quite ready to rest.
I was sick of greeting an empty house.
In any case we thought we might go back
When school was ended. We celebrated
The loss of the job buying a hot, red
Dress for her and stepping out to dinner.
We had one of those concoctions of wined
Meat sizzling on a stick to be eaten
Piece at a time with salad of lucid
Geometrically beautiful bam-
boo slices. I knew better than order
The oily chicken and rice with chopsticks.
There's an incommensurable ratio
Between a chopstick and a grain of rice,
And a Chinese chicken wants pots of tea.
Later we went to the Honolulu
Art Gallery: we heard a local group
Play quartets and looked at the tropical
Fish mugging in the intermission. Much
Better than the Waikiki movie spot
With its real coconut palms looming up
On either side of a screened Oberon
Or Cary Grant. Somehow I could not get
Used to that, or to the military
Colonies inside of their volcanoes,
The new screams inside Honolulu's zoo,
The powerfully beautiful Pali
View, with land dropping rapidly away
A thousand feet and following in miles
Wide patterns to the sea. I dream of this,
And of another view over downtown
Honolulu from the Heights where I sat
With Ruth in an Hawaiian shade and read
The Oxford Book of Christian Verse. At left

Was a sheer fall and stream and then a great
Field behind King Kamehameha's tomb.
Ruth and I had lain at night in the grass
Behind Kamehameha's bones and his
Relic arms, and saw the planes pass to East:
After a native feast—pig in a pit
At a luau, with raw fish, raw whiskey,
Raw seaweed on the side, and gray, bland poi
Dipped with the hand—a party for a boy
From school. His family presented Ruth
With a brilliant, Chinese-black, lacquered bowl
Full of pineapple, freshly cut with salt,
Barely moist, a most delicate yellow.
Ruth's red lacquer dress was paid for after
Several days in those pineapple fields.
Everybody, students and teachers both,
Simply took off to help in the harvest.
There was a pretty dilapidated-
Looking, empty-looking water tower
In the field—it was no barrel of fun
And neither was the job. You don't forget
The terrible heat on the storm helmets
Over the thorn leaves of the pineapples.
They're not so gentle as the mango is
(Or, for a tree, as is the tamarisk).
Once I went on a trip with the school of
Botany at the University.
We left our ten cars and walked off all roads
Slushing through the fields of clay and over
Sluices way up into the lifting hills.
Each one you see of a certain kind of
Tree is a different variety:
Something to do with rain forests, they say.
It didn't stay dry very long that day!
Those trees lose their years for they form no rings
To reckon in this eternal season.
It has no hour. I saw the exciting
Passion flower, that smells of burning flesh,
Taking on the shape and colors of a
Tropical bird, surrealist, absurd.
I loved the trees of sandalwood. They made
The merchants rich; they were carried in ships
To England for incense and then later

Were banned from the island for some reason
Or banned from the Orient or else went
Largely extinct. I forget. Was it burnt
All off in a tropical forest fire?
I am sure the branches of certain trees
Contain so much pitch they will flame for hours
As the naked men, wet skin torchlit, by
The sea's blackened edge, swing out their big, white
Billowing net, and spill its thousand fish.
Evenings on board ship the best part of the
Trip. Clouds catching several lights of sea
And those of the losing sun, and scudding
At times like bunches of scrubbed wool with soft,
Trapped light about the sky. When we arrived
Late at night the island lay like money
In the story on the velvet prince's
Pouch, or like drops of rain upon the tongue
Of a black flower. My god how it rained
On the field trip! . . . No place in those high spots
To cover up. You know the rain will last
And you have to get back. You single track
So as not to separate and be drowned.
You crush a while in a futile kind of
Trial against a bank, but soon or late:
You agree to soak. Occasionally
I stopped in that wet to collect some moss
For a friend in an Iowa college.
A coed helped. The immodest effect
Of the rain on her particularly
Hit me. I thought her blouse clinging to her
Small breasts well worth remembering. I left
All my moss in our Honolulu house
That last wild day on the island. We went
Because there wasn't any winter there.
We had trouble getting reservations;
But found some on the Matson through a friend
Of mine, a Buddhist, business aide at school.
He had a contact at the ocean line.
The liturgy was done with perfect art
At Convent of the Sacred Heart. The priest
Gave a homily that was to the point,
And the chants of nuns were never human.

On Mayday hundreds of Hawaiian girls
In uniform crowned the Blessed Virgin
While the nuns' house was open, and every
Body sang on the lawn. The convent gate
Gave access to the sisters in their clouds
Of woolen white, a perfect, needle point-
ed bleeding heart under an ageless face.
We talked to one when she was stopped for rest.
She had huge moles with shining hairs on her
Chaucerian countenance. The ancient
Face of sky changed and changed at night. I watched
Figures of ballet slow and settle there
In puffs of powder. We lolled one night late
Outside the music room and heard a Swan
Lake tide and fall by the island rock wall.
One night's noon saw the odd moon flower bloom
Beside the school at Punahou. I thought
Of were-wolves' London whines. At school recess
Boys played the ukulele and the girls
Always wore hibiscus in their hair. Those
Boys loved quite young, and all day long they rode
Surf in the summer sun. Waves knock, and gun.
Ruth was far gone in the malaise that gives
Life to men: that last day was mean for her.
She was a little green as we were kissed
In our cabin by friends who gave tear full,
Fragrant leis of ginger and of jasmine.
Strawberry guavas were good or better
Than gooseberries I remembered at home.
I hunted them when I went for lessons
On the piano. The teacher played flute
In the chamber group at the gallery.
There were guavas by the light, quiet spot
Where I got off the late afternoon bus.
Children were way down the block, and the sun
Slanted in the special air. Enough rain
To have it fresh to breathe. I had trouble,
Because of envy, with a sonata
Brahms wrote at twenty. As the ship pulled out
From under the pier's high clock, I thought that
I had not said goodbye to my teacher.
The charming, muscular children still run

For gold in the quick, bright wake of the ship,
Their breech cloths blowing in the waters' air
Like feathers of Hawaiian birds up there
Before the rain. But all the birds were dead
In Bishop's museum. I for my part
Cared more for the Polynesian village
In the court. I liked the snails that became
Extinct when their shells curved into a spi-
ral six feet across and equal angled.
And once a colony of good kids flowed
Past a dusty glass case, all fully dressed.
They took some kind of notes. And now they dove
About the wake and were lost, and now they
Broke again and grinned with lips of shocking
Color I had seen off Diamond Head
From a glass bottomed boat, their teeth like
Stunning shells that have sunned on the sea's steps.
There are certain shapes in the deeper sea
And certain exquisite tones in the dark
There where light never goes. I think these kids
Were bright as those shapes. I am sure they shrieked
In a gaudy English. The gulf grew wide
And Ruth and I had our picture taken
By the rail. Our hair blew to Hawaii.
The flowers around our necks all stayed fresh
In that picture, no more changed than the land
Marking mountain in the background; a bus
In the road at its foot waits for passage
Like a vassal at the palace. I know
How beautiful the sea is on this side
Of that road: many-colored marvelous
High poundings, caught a moment before spilling
In that particular light, had held
Me all one Sunday. The picnic sand was
Pointed and wet on the skin of my back.
I took Ruth's hand. We walked on the beach and
Found a stream hid away from there. We crossed
A fence. We felt it wasn't meant for us.
We did not trespass, for there was some spring
Or source to find we thought, and we moved
Around the side of a lower mountain
Along that stream. At this angle, though not

From the road or beach, above the level
Of the shade, a thin waterfall sudden-
ly dropped before us, as colorful tears
The acacia trees cry down from their tops
On the hill. This beauty was unsupposed.
There was no one about! Along the bank
Of the stream small shells lay, passing much light,
Brought in some way out of the bright sea. I
Loved Ruth in this place. Ruth loved me. We found
Our son beside that stream in that now
Alien heaven. We have not told him.
Perhaps he'll come upon it in himself
Someday to make lucid some mystery
About his midwest youth. To look back and
Find that! . . . The long unknown wisps of water
Dropped from tropical woods where sandalwood
Smells so sweet and burns so bird bright, and then
Gone in to the musculine sea where immense
Tunas tremble off the shore and small
Devil fish, a brilliant blue in the sand,
Die with malice and sting the bone white feet.
I ran over the stone, wet beach at night
My first trip around the island past Di-
amond Head. I was alone. I stripped and
Left my clothes in the borrowed jeep. That fresh
Nakedness in another world was good.
I fell on the shore out of human breath
And I smelled in that damp sand sandalwood
And faint bits of fish borne from the agèd
East which I was closer to, separate
Only by the long, slow movements of the
Deeper sea that touched my face now and skin
With its own tide, and I felt under my
Shivering chest and belly and under
My Iowa loins, ancient Polyne-
sian grains blown from the sea, the fertile rice
Of a great and furious race. At last
I stood quiet by that fathering sea.
From its iridescent froth a golden
Flying fish winged and rose in front of me
Into a weightless arch, and at the end
Went again into it. The whitening

Wake of our ship spread with the better speed
And I saw in it the arcs of fireworks
At New Year rocketing in the valley
Below as we watched from our window. Ruth
Had been so startled at the lack of snow.
I did not mind there were no fallen leaves.
It was Ruth who missed the season, and I?
I would have missed her had I stayed. Better
A short time, I thought, as the ship moved out;
After all, the trees are not my trees. The
Obscene breadfruit which they say the natives
Used to eat. The exhibitionistic
Hibiscus. The austere eucalyptus
With provoking oil and tattered grey.
The papaya is not right on the west-
ern palate. But the mimosa tree, so
Sensitive it shrinks to the limb at touch
Of its tip, one could feel inside the heart.
I hoped I had forgot the gnarled village-
like, cavernous banyan tree on the lawn
At Kamehameha's Palace, where the
Hundred thousand feathers on official plumes
And hats gather dust: they had been picked
From those fields of birds. Our Buddhist friend
Will not allow us to forget *Ficus*,
The Fig, where Buddha sat at the center
In the world, as its quivering leaves tell.
Perhaps the last sound we heard as the space
To Hawaii grew great was the clapping
Of the Buddhist boards as from the temple
On our hill—waking us at four o'clock,
Clattering from time to time through the day.
One Sunday, waked by that, I walked beyond
The school to a lucent, deep rock-lined pool;
I swam as the boards clacked and the tinny
Cymbals clanged their morning prayers; and I sat
A while, my legs crossed upon the pool's ledge.
I knew I was too narrow for a god.
I thought the tone of Buddhist funeral
Reeds better suited me. Later I looked
At the awesome inside of a temple.
The brass and gold of the great canopy!

The brilliant, occult lights! I found their book
Inside the pew and said a Buddhist act
Of faith and thought about our friend who helped.
He also served the priest and taught holy
Wrestling to the young; an ancient kind of
Champion, a powerful, neckbreaking
Man, a great Chinese who's solid as his
Ancestral wall, and who revered the foods
I would not eat. There was no job to miss
On board the ship, but you could go to Mass.
The trip was terrible for Ruth. We went
First class. She could not eat the likeable
Squab under glass. We read Sigrid Undset
Out loud on the deck in the better airs.
Now home, we have our trees and seasons'
Change and our own, unmixed, midwest prayers.

A TRIP TO FOUR OR FIVE TOWNS

To James Wright

1

The gold-colored skin of my Lebanese friends.
Their deep, lightless eyes.
The serene, inner, careful
balance they share. The conjugal
smile of either for either.

2

This bellychilling, shoe soaking, factory-
dug-up-hill smothering Pittsburgh weather!
I wait for a cab in the smart mahogany
lobby of the seminary.
The marble *Pietà* is flanked around
with fake fern. She cherishes her dead son
stretched along her womb he triple crossed.
A small, slippered priest
pads up. Whom do you seek, my son?
Father, I've come in out of the rain.
I seek refuge from the elemental tears,
for my heavy, earthen body runs to grief
and I am apt to drown

in this small and underhanded rain
that drops its dross so delicately
on the hairs of the flowers, my father,
and follows down the veins of leaves
weeping quiet in the wood.

My yellow cab never came,
but I did not confess
beneath the painted Jesus Christ. I left
and never saved myself at all
That night in that late, winter rain.

3

In Washington, was it spring?
I took the plane.
I heard, on either side,
the soft executives, manicured and
fat, fucking this and fucking that.
My heavy second breakfast
lay across my lap.
At port, in the great concourse,
I could not walk to city bus
or cab? or limousine?
I sweat with shock, with havoc
Of the hundred kinds of time,
trembling like a man away from home.

At the National Stripshow
where the girls wriggle right
and slow, I find I want to see in
under the sequin stepin.
And in my later dream of the negro girl's room
strong with ancient sweat and with her thick
aroma, I seem to play a melodrama
as her great, red dog barks twice
and I stab it with my pocket knife.

4

In Richmond the azalea banks
burst in rose and purple gullies by the car,
muted in the soft, wet
April twilight. The old estates

were pruned and rolled fresh
with spring, with splendor, touching
the graceful stride of the boy who brings the paper.

5

My friend has a red-headed mother
capable of love in any kind
of weather. I am not sure
what she passes to her daughters
but from her brown eye and from her breast
she passes wit and spunk to her big sons.
And she is small and pleased when they put
their arms around her, having caught her.
They cut the grass naked to the waist.
They cure the handsome skins of chipmunks and of snakes.
And when they wake in their attic room
they climb down the ladder, half
asleep, feeling the rungs' pressure
on their bare feet, shirt tails out,
brown eyes shut. They eat
what she cooks. One shot a gorgeous colored hawk
and posed with it, proud, arms and full wings
spread. And one, at the beach,
balanced on his hands, posed
stripped, in the void of sand,
limbs a rudder in the wind,
amid the lonely, blasted wood.
And two sons run swift roans in the high, summer grass.
Now I would guess
her daughters had at least this same
grace and beauty as their mother,
though I have only seen their picture.
I know she is happy with her three
strong sons about her, for they are not clumsy
(one, calmed, so calmly,
bends a good ear to his guitar)
and they are not dull:
one built a small electric shaft topped with a glowing ball.

6

In New York I got drunk, to tell the truth,
and almost got locked up when a beat

friend with me took a leak in a telephone booth.
(E. E. Cummings on the Paris lawn.
"Reprieve pisseur Américain!")
At two o'clock he got knocked out
horning in with the girl in the room over him.
Her boy friend was still sober,
and too thin. I saw the blood of a poet
flow on the sidewalk. Oh, if I mock,
it is without heart. I thought
of the torn limbs of Orpheus
scattered in the grass on the hills of Thrace.
Do poets have to have such trouble with the female race?
I do not know. But if they bleed
I lose heart also.
When he reads, ah, when he reads, small but deep voiced,
he reads well: now weeps, now is cynical,
his large, horned eyes very black and tearful.

And when we visited a poet father
we rode to Jersey on a motor scooter.
My tie and tweeds looped in the winds.
I choked in the wake
of the Holland Pipe, and cops,
under glass like carps, eyed us.
That old father was so mellow and generous —
easy to pain,
white, open and at peace, and of good taste,
Like his Rutherford house.
And he read, very loud and regal,
sixteen new poems based on paintings by Brueghel!

7
The last night out,
before I climbed on the formal
Capital Viscount and was shot home
high, pure and clear,
seemed like the right time
to disappear.

June, 1959

S. S. Gardons

THE SURVIVORS

We wondered what might change
Once you were not here;
Tried to guess how they would rearrange
Their life, now you were dead. Oh, it was strange
Coming back this year—

To find the lawn unkept
And the rock gardens dense
With bindweed; the tangling rosebushes crept
And squandered over everything except
The trash thrown by the fence;

The rose trellises blown
Down and still sprawled there;
Broken odd ends of porch furniture thrown
Around the yard; everything overgrown
Or down in disrepair.

On the tree they still protect
From the ungoverned gang
Of neighbor boys,—eaten with worms, bird-pecked,
But otherwise uncared-for and unpicked,
The bitter cherries hang,

Brown and soft and botched.
The ground is thick with flies.
Around in front, two white stone lions are crouched
By the front steps; someone has patched
Cement across their eyes.

The Venetian blinds are drawn;
Inside, it is dark and still.
Always upon some errand, one by one,
They go from room to room, vaguely, in the wan
Half-light, deprived of will.

Mostly they hunt for some-
thing they've misplaced; otherwise
They turn the pages of magazines and hum
Tunelessly. At any time they come
To pass, they drop their eyes.

Only at night they meet.
By voiceless summoning
They come to the livingroom; each repeats
Some words he has memorized; each takes his seat
In the hushed, expectant ring

By the television set.
No one can draw his eyes
From that unnatural, cold light. They wait.
The screen goes dim; they huddle closer yet,
As the image dies.

In the cellar where the sewers
Rise, unseen, the pale white
Ants grow in decaying stacks of old newspapers.
Outside, street lamps appear; old friends of yours
Call children in for the night.

And you have been dead one year.
Nothing is different here.

FOURTH OF JULY

The drifting smoke is gone, today,
From the mill chimneys; the laborers from the great
Iron foundries are on strike. They celebrate
Their Independence her own way.

She stopped a year ago today.
Firecrackers mark the occasion down the street;
I thumb through magazines and keep my seat.
What can anybody say?

In her room, nights, we lie awake
By racks of unworn party dresses, shoes,
Her bedside asthma pipe, the glasses whose
Correction no one else will take.

Stuffed dogs look at us from the shelf
When we sit down together at the table.
You put a face on things the best you're able
And keep your comments to yourself.

It is a hideous mistake.
My young wife, unforgivably alive,
Takes a deep breath and blows out twenty-five
Candles on her birthday cake.

It is agreed she'll get her wish.
The candles smell; smoke settles through the room
Like a cheap stage set for Juliet's tomb.
I leave my meal cold on the dish.

We take the children to the park
To watch the fireworks and the marching band.
For hours a drill team pivots at command.
For hours we sit in the dark

Hearing some politician fume;
Someone leads out a blond schoolgirl to crown
Queen of this war-contract factory town;
Skyrockets and the last guns boom.

I keep my seat and wonder where,
Into what ingrown nation has she gone
Among a people silent and withdrawn;
I wonder in the stifling air

Of what deprived and smoke-filled town
They brush together and do not feel lust,
Hope, rage, love; within what senseless dust
Is she at home to settle down;

Where do they know her, and the dead
Meet in a vacancy of shared disgrace,
Keep an old holiday of blame and place
Their tinsel wreath on her dark head?

We tramp home through the sulfurous smoke
That is my father's world. Now we must
Enter my mother's house of lint and dust
She could not breathe; I wheeze and choke.

It is an evil, stupid joke;
My wife is pregnant; my sister's in her grave.
We live in the home of the free and of the brave.
No one would hear me, even if I spoke.

Kenneth Koch

AUS EINER KINDHEIT

Is the basketball coach a homosexual lemon manufacturer?
    It is suspected by O'Ryan in his submarine.
When I was a child we always cried to be driven for a ride
    in that submarine. Daddy would say Yes!
Mommy would say No! The maid read *Anna Karenina* and
    told us secrets. Some suspected her of a liaison
    with O'Ryan. Nothing but squirrels
Seemed to be her interest, at the windows, except on
    holidays, like Easter and Thanksgiving, when
She would leave the basement and rave among the leaves,
    shouting, I am the Spirit of Softball! Come to me!
Daddy would always leave town. And a chorus of spiders
Would hang from my bedroom wall. Mommy had a hat
    made out of pasty hooks. She gave a party to
    limburger cheese.
We all were afraid that O'Ryan would come!
He came, he came! as the fall wind comes, waving and
    razing and swirling the leaves
With his bags, his moustache, his cigar, his golfball, his
    pencils, his April compasses, and over his whole
Body we children saw signs of life beneath the water! Oh!
Will he dance the hornpipe? we wondered, Will he smoke
    a cigar underneath eleven inches of ocean? Will he
    beat the pavement
Outside our door with his light feet, for being so firm? Is he
    a lemon Memnon?
O'Ryan O'Ryan O'Ryan! The maid came up from the
    basement, we were all astonished. And she said, "Is
    it Thanksgiving? Christmas? I felt
A force within me stir." And then she saw O'Ryan! The
    basketball coach followed her up from the cellar.
    He and O'Ryan fight!
No one is homosexual then! happily I swim through the
    bath-tubs with my scarlet-haired sister
Z. ("O women I love you!" O'Ryan cried.) And we parked
    under water. Then, looking out the window

We saw that snow had begun to fall, upon the green grass,
     and both shyly entered the new world of our
     bleached underwear. Rome! Rome!
Was our maid entertaining that limburger cheese, or my
     mother? has the passageway fallen asleep? and can
     one's actions for six years be called "improper"?
I hope not. I hope the sea. I hope cigars will be smoked.
     I hope it from New York to California. From
     Tallahassee to St. Paul.
I hope the orange punching bag will be socked, and that
     you'll be satisfied, sweet friend. I hope international
     matrimony, lambent skies, and "Ship, ahoy!"
For we're due to be dawned on, I guess.

TAKING A WALK WITH YOU

My misunderstandings: for years I thought "muso bello"
     meant "Bell Muse," I thought it was a kind of
Extra reward on the slotmachine of my shyness in the snow
     when
February was only a bouncing ball before the Hospital of
     the Two Sisters of the Last
Hamburger Before I Go to Sleep. I thought Axel's Castle
     was a garage;
And I had beautiful dreams about it, too—sensual,
     mysterious mechanisms; horns honking, wheels
     turning . . .
My misunderstandings were:
1] thinking Pinocchio could really change from a puppet
     into a real boy, and back again!
2] thinking it depended on whether he was good or bad!
3] identifying him with myself!
4] and therefore every time I was bad being afraid I
     would turn into wood . . .
5] I misunderstood childhood. I usually liked the age I
     was. However, now I regard twenty-nine as an
     optimum age (for me).
6] I disliked Shelly between twenty and twenty-five.
All of these things I suppose are understandable, but
When you were wearing your bodice I did not understand
     that you had nothing beneath it;

When my father turned the corner I misunderstood the
　　light very much
On Fifty-fifth Street; and I misunderstood (like an old
　　Chinese restaurant) what he was doing there.
I misunderstand generally Oklahoma and Arkansas, though
　　I think I understand New Mexico;
I understand the Painted Desert, cowboy hats, and vast
　　spaces; I do
Not understand hillbilly life—I am sure I misunderstand it.
I did not understand that you had nothing on beneath
　　your bodice
Nor, had I understood this, would I have understood what
　　it meant; even now I
(Merry Christmas! Here, Father, take your package)
　　misunderstand it!
Merry Christmas, Uncle Leon! yes, here is your package
　　too.

I misunderstand Renaissance life; I misunderstand:
The Renaissance;
Ancient China;
The Middle Atlantic States and what they are like;
The tubes of London and what they mean;
Titian, Michelangelo, Vermeer;
The origins of words;
What others are talking about;
Music from the beginnings to the present time;
Laughter; and tears, even more so;
Value (economic and esthetic);
Snow (and weather in the country);
The meaning of the symbols and myths of Christmas.
I misunderstand you,
I misunderstand the day we walked down the street
　　together for ten hours—
Where were we going? I had thought we were going
　　somewhere. I believe I misunderstand many of the
　　places we passed and things you said . . .
I misunderstand "Sons of Burgundy,"
I misunderstand that you had nothing painted beneath
　　your bodice,
I misunderstand "Notification of Arrival or Departure
　　to Be Eradicated Before Affection of Deceased
　　Tenant."

I understand that
The smoke and the clouds are both a part of the day, but

I misunderstand the words "After Departure,"
I misunderstand nothingness;
I misunderstand the attitude of people in pharmacies, on
    the decks of ships, in my bedroom, amid the pine
    needles, on mountains of cotton, everywhere—
When they say paralytic I hear parasite, and when they say
    coffee I think music . . .
What is wrong with me from head to toe
That I misinterpret everything I hear? I misunderstand:
French: often;
Italian: sometimes, almost always—for example, if
    someone says, "Fortunate ones!" I am likely to
    think he is referring to the fountain with the blue
    and red water (I am likely to make this mistake also
    in English).
I misunderstand Greek entirely;
I find ancient Greece very hard to understand: I probably
    misunderstand it;
I misunderstand spoken German about 98% of the time,
    like the cathedral in the middle of a town;
I misunderstand "Beautiful Adventures"; I also think I
    probably misunderstand *La Nausée* by Jean-Paul
    Sartre . . .
I probably misunderstand misunderstanding itself—I
    misunderstand the Via Margutta in Rome, or Via
    della Vite, no matter what street, all of them.
I misunderstand wood in the sense of its relationship to
    the tree; I misunderstand people who take one
    attitude or another about it . . .
Spring I would like to say I understand, but I most
    probably don't—autumn, winter, and summer are
    all in the same boat
(Ruined ancient cities by the sea).

I misunderstand *vacation* and *umbrella*,
I misunderstand *motion* and *weekly*
(Though I think I understand "Daytime Pissarros"
And the octagon—I do not understand the public
    garden) . . .

Oh I am sure there is a use for all of them, but what is it?
My misunderstandings confuse Rome and Ireland, and
      can you
Bring that beautiful sex to bear upon it?
I misunderstand what I am saying, though not to you;
I misunderstand a large boat: that is a ship.
What you are feeling for me I misunderstand totally; I
      think I misunderstand the very possibilities of
      feeling,
Especially here in Rome, where I somehow think I am.
I see the sky, and sails.
(I misunderstand the mustard and the bottle)
Oh that we could go sailing in that sky!
What tune came with the refreshments?
I am unable to comprehend why they were playing off key.
Is it because they wanted us to jump over the cliff
Or was one of them a bad or untrained musician
Or the whole lot of them?
At any rate
San Giovanni in Laterano
Also resisted my questioning
And turned a deaf blue dome to me
Far too successfully.

I cannot understand why you walk forwards and
      backwards with me.
I think it is because you want to try out your shoes for
      their toes.
It is Causation that is my greatest problem
And after that the really attentive study of millions of
      details.

I love you, but it is difficult to stop writing.
As a flea could write the Divine Comedy of a water jug.
      Now Irish mists close in upon us.
Peat sails through the air, and greenness becomes bright.
      Are you the ocean or the island? Am I on Irish soil,
      or are your waves covering me?
St. Peter's bells are ringing: "Earthquake, inundation, and
      sleep to the understanding!"
(American Express! flower vendors! your beautiful straight
      nose! that delightful trattoria in Santa Maria in
      Trastevere!)

Let us have supper at Santa Maria in Trastevere
Where by an absolute and total misunderstanding (but
        not fatal) I once ate before I met you.
I am probably misinterpreting your answer, since I hear
        nothing, and I believe I am alone.

THE ARTIST

Ah, well, I abandon you, cherrywood smokestack,
Near the entrance to this old green park! . . .

                                *

Cherrywood avalanche, my statue of you
Is still standing in Toledo, Ohio.
O places, summer, boredom, the static of an acrobatic
        blue!

And I made an amazing zinc airliner
It is standing to this day in the Minneapolis zoo . . .

Old times are not so long ago, plaster-of-paris haircut!

                                *

I often think *Play* was my best work.
It is an open field with a few boards in it.

Children are allowed to come and play in Play
By permission of the Cleveland Museum.
I look up at the white clouds, I wonder what I shall do, and
        smile.

Perhaps somebody will grow up having been influenced
        by *Play*,
I think—but what good will that do?
Meanwhile I am interested in steel cigarettes . . .

                                *

The orders are coming in thick and fast for steel cigarettes,
        steel cigars.

The Indianapolis Museum has requested six dozen
    packages,
I wonder if I'd still have the courage to do a thing like
    Play?

I think I may go to Cleveland . . .

*

Well, here I am! Pardon me, can you tell me how to get to
    the Cleveland Museum's monumental area, *Play?*

"Mister, that was torn down a long time ago. You ought
    to go and see the new thing they have now—*Gun.*"
What? *Play* torn down?
"Yes, Mister, and I loved to climb in it too, when I was a
    kid!" And he shakes his head
Sadly . . . But I am thrilled beyond expectation!
He liked my work!
And I guess there must be others like that man in
    Cleveland too . . .

So you see, *Play* has really had its effect!
Now I am on the outskirts of town
And . . . here it is! But it has changed! There are some
    blue merds lying in the field
And it's not marked *Play* anymore—and here's a calf!
I'm so happy, I can't tell why!
Was this how I originally imagined *Play*, but lacked the
    courage?

It would be hard now, though, to sell it to another
    museum.
I wonder if the man I met's children will come and play
    in it?
How does one's audience survive?

*

Pittsburgh, May 16th. I have abandoned the steel
    cigarettes. I am working on *Bee*.
Bee will be a sixty-yards-long covering for the elevator
    shaft opening in the foundry sub-basement
Near my home. So far it's white sailcloth with streams of
    golden paint evenly spaced out

With a small blue pond at one end, and around it orange
        and green flowers. My experience in Cleveland
        affected me so
That my throat aches whenever I am not working at full
        speed. I have never been so happy and inspired and
Play seems to me now like a juvenile experience!

*

June 8th. *Bee* is still not finished. I have introduced a huge
        number of red balloons into it. How will it work?
Yesterday X. said, "Are you still working on *Bee?* What's
        happened to your interest in steel cigarettes?"
Y. said, "He hasn't been doing any work at all on them
        since he went to Cleveland." A shrewd guess! But
        how much can they possibly know?

*

November 19th. Disaster! *Bee* was almost completed, and
        now the immense central piece of sailcloth has torn.
        Impossible to repair it!

December 4th. I've gone back to work on *Bee!* I suddenly
        thought (after weeks of despair!), "I can place the
        balloons over the tear in the canvas!" So that is
        what I am doing. All promises to be well!

December 6th. The foreman of the foundry wants to look
        at my work. It seems that he too is an "artist" —
        does sketches and watercolors and such . . . What
        will he think of *Bee?*

*

Cherrywood! I had left you far from my home
And the foreman came to look at *Bee*
And the zinc airliner flew into *Play!*

The pink balloons aren't heavy, but the yellow ones break
The foreman says, "It's the greatest thing I ever saw!"
Cleveland heard too and wants me to come back and
        reinaugurate *Play*

I dream of going to Cleveland but never will
Bee has obsessed my mind.

*

March 14th. A cold spring day. It is snowing. *Bee* is
completed.

*

O *Bee* I think you are my best work
In the blue snow-filled air
I feel my heart break

I lie down in the snow
They come from the foundry and take *Bee* away
Oh what can I create now, Earth,

Green Earth on which everything blossoms anew?
"A bathroom floor cardboard trolley line
The shape and size of a lemon seed with on the inside
A passenger the size of a pomegranate seed
Who is an invalid and has to lean on the cardboard side
Of the lemon-seed-sized trolley line so that he won't fall
off the train."

*

I just found these notes written many years ago.
How seriously I always take myself! Let it be a lesson
to me.
To bring things up to date: I have just finished *Campaign,*
which is a tremendous piece of charcoal.
Its shape is difficult to describe; but it is extremely large
and would reach to the sixth floor of the Empire
State Building. I have been very successful in the
past fourteen or fifteen years.

*

Summer Night, shall I never succeed in finishing you? Oh
you are the absolute end of all my creation! The
ethereal beauty of that practically infinite number
of white stone slabs stretching into the blue secrecy
of ink! O stabs in my heart!

. . . . Why not a work *Stabs in My Heart?* But *Summer
Night?*

January . . . . A troubled sleep. Can I make two things
at once? What way is there to be sure that the
impulse to work on *Stabs in My Heart* is serious?

It seems occasioned only by my problem about finishing *Summer Night* . . . . ?

*

The *Magician of Cincinnati* is now ready for human use. They are twenty-five tremendous stone staircases, each over six hundred feet high, which will be placed in the Ohio River between Cincinnati and Louisville, Kentucky. All the boats coming down the Ohio River will presumably be smashed up against the immense statues, which are the most recent work of the creator of *Flowers, Bee, Play, Again* and *Human Use.* Five thousand citizens are thronged on the banks of the Ohio waiting to see the installation of the work, and the crowd is expected to be more than fifteen times its present number before morning. There will be a game of water baseball in the early afternoon, before the beginning of the ceremonies, between the Cincinnati Redlegs and the Pittsburgh Pirates. The *Magician of Cincinnati,* incidentally, is said to be absolutely impregnable to destruction of any kind, and will therefore presumably always be a feature of this part of Ohio . . .

*

May 16th. With what an intense joy I watched the installation of the *Magician of Cincinnati* today, in the Ohio River, where it belongs, and which is so much a part of my original scheme . . .

May 17th. I feel suddenly freed from life—not so much as if my work were going to change, but as though I had at last seen what I had so long been prevented (perhaps I prevented myself) from seeing: that there is too much for me to do. Somehow this enables me to relax, to breathe easily . . .

*

There's the *Magician of Cincinnati*
In the distance
Here I am in the green trees of Pennsylvania

How strange I felt when they had installed
The *Magician!* . . . Now a bluebird trills, I am busy
    making my polished stones
For *Dresser*.

The stream the stone the birds the reddish-pink
    Pennsylvania hills
All go to make up *Dresser*
Why am I camping out?
I am waiting for the thousand of tons of embalming fluid
That have to come and with which I can make these hills.

*

GREATEST ARTISTIC EVENT HINTED BY GOVERNOR
Reading, June 4. Greatest artistic event was hinted today
    by governor. Animals converge on meadow where
    artist working.

CONVERGE ON MEADOW WHERE WORKING

ARTIST HINTED, SAME MAN

. . . . the *Magician of Cincinnati*

THREE YEARS

October 14th. I want these hills to be striated! How naïve
    the *Magician of Cincinnati* was! Though it makes
    me happy to think of it . . . Here, I am plunged
    into such real earth! Striate, hills! What is this
    deer's head of green stone? I can't fabricate
    anything less than what I think should girdle the
    earth . . .

PHOTOGRAPH
PHOTOGRAPH
PHOTOGRAPH

Artist who created the *Magician of Cincinnati*; Now at
    work in
Pennsylvania; The Project—*Dresser*—So Far.

*

Ah! . . . .

*

TONS

SILICON, GRASS AND DEER-HEAD RANGE

Philadelphia. Your voice as well as mine will be appreciated to express the appreciation of *Dresser*, which makes of Pennsylvania the silicon, grass and stone deer-head center of the world . . . Artist says he may change his mind about the central bridges. Fountains to give forth real tarwater. Mountain lake in center. Real chalk cliffs. Also cliffs of clay. Deep declivities nearby. "Wanted forest atmosphere, yet to be open." Gas . . .

*

PHOTOGRAPH

SKETCH

DEDICATION CEREMONY

GOES SWIMMING IN OWN STREAM

SHAKING HANDS WITH GOVERNOR

COLOR PICTURE

THE HEAD OF THE ARTIST

THE ARTIST'S HAND

STACK OF ACTUAL BILLS NEEDED TO PAY FOR PROJECT

Story of *Dresser*

PENNSYLVANIA'S PRIDE: *DRESSER*

Creator of *Dresser*

*

STILL SMILING AT FORGE

Beverly, South Dakota, April 18. Still smiling at forge, artist of *Dresser* says, "No, of course I haven't forgotten *Dresser*. Though how quickly the years have gone since I have been doing *Too!*" We glanced up at the sky and saw a large white bird, somewhat similar to an immense seagull, which was as if fixed above our heads. Its eyes were blue sapphires, and its wings were formed by an ingenious arrangement of whitened daffodil-blossom parts. Its body seemed mainly charcoal, on the whole, with a good deal of sand mixed in. As we watched it, the creature actually seemed to move . . .

*

August 4th. . . . Three four five, and it's finished! I can
　　see it in Beverly . . .

*

BEVERLY HONORS ARTIST. CALLED "FOUNDING
　FATHER"
Beverly, South Dakota, August 14 . . .
MISSISSIPPI CLAIMS BIRTHPLACE
HONORS BIRTHPLACE
BIRTHPLACE HONORS HELD

*

INDIANS AND SAVANTS MEET TO PRAISE *WEST WIND*
PAT HONORED
PAT AND *WEST WIND* HONORED

*

June 3rd. It doesn't seem possible—the Pacific Ocean! I
　　have ordered sixteen million tons of blue paint.
　　Waiting anxiously for it to arrive. How would grass
　　be as a substitute? cement?

*

GEOGRAPHY

1

In the blue hubbub of the same-through-wealth sky
Amba grew to health and fifteenth year among the jungle
　　scrubbery.
The hate-bird sang on a lower wing of the birch-nut tree
And Amba heard him sing, and in his health he too
Began to sing, but then stopped. Along the lower Congo
There are such high plants of what there is there, when
At morning Amba heard their pink music as gentlemanly
As if he had been in civilization. When morning stank
Over the ridge of coconuts and bald fronds, with agility
Amba climbed the permanent nut trees, and will often
　　sing
To the shining birds, and the pets in their stealth

Are each other among, also, whether it be blue (thhhh)
     feathers
Or green slumber. Africa in Amba's mind was those white
     mornings he sang
(thhhh) high trala to the nougat birds, and after
The trenches had all been dug for the day, Amba
Would dream at the edge of some stained and stinking
     pond
Of the afternight music, as blue pets came to him in his
     dreams;
From the orange coconuts he would extract some stained
     milk,
Underneath his feet roots, tangled and filthy green. At
     night
The moon (zzzzzz) shining down on Amba's sweet
     mocked sleep.

2

In Chicago Louis walked the morning's rounds with
     agility.
A boy of seventeen and already recognized as a fast
     milkman!
The whizz and burr of dead chimes oppressed the
Holocaustic unison of Frank's brain, a young outlaw
Destined to meet dishonor and truth in a same instant,
Crossing Louis' path gently in the street, the great secret
     unknown.

3

The fur rhubarb did not please Daisy. "Freddie," she
     called,
"Our fruit's gang mouldy." Daisy, white cheeks with a
     spot of red
In them, like apples grown in paper bags, smiled
Gently at the fresh new kitchen; and, then, depressed,
She began to cover the rhubarb with her hands.

4

In the crushy green ice and snow Baba ran up and around
     with exuberance!
Today, no doubt, Father and Uncle Dad would come, and
     together they three would chase the whale!
Baba stared down through the green crusty ice at the
     world of fish

And closed his eyes and began to imagine the sweet trip
Over the musky waters, when Daddy would spear the
  whale, and the wind
Blow "Crad, crad!" through Uncle Dad's fur, and the
  sweet end
Of the day where they would smile at one another over
  the smoking blubber,
And Uncle Dad would tell tales of his adventures past the
  shadow bar
Chasing the white snow-eagle. Baba ran
Into the perfect igloo screaming with impatience, and
  Malmal,
His mother, kissed him and dressed him with loving care
  for the icy trip.

5

Ten Ko sprinted over the rice paddies. Slush, slosh, sloosh!
His brother, Wan Kai, would soon be returned from the
  village
Where he had gone . . . (Blue desire! . . .)

6

Roon startled her parents by appearing perfectly dressed
In a little white collar and gown.
Angebor lifted himself up so he might stare in the window
  at the pretty girl.
His little hands unclenched and dropped the coins he had
  saved for the *oona*.
He opened wide his eyes, then blinked at the pretty little
  girl. He had never seen anything like that.
That evening, when it whitened in the sky, and a green
Clearness was there, Maggia and Angebor had no *oona*.
But Angebor talked with excitement of what he had seen,
  and Maggia drank *zee'th*.

7

The little prisoner wept and wailed, telling of his life in
  the sand
And the burning sun over the desert. And one night it was
  cool
And dark, and he stole away over the green sand to search
  for his parents.
And he went to their tent, and they kissed him and
  covered him with loving-kindness.

And the new morning sun shone like a pink rose in the
    heavens,
And the family prayed, the desert wind scorching their
    cool skin.

8

Amba arose. Thhhhhhh! went the birds, and clink clank
    cleck went
The leaves under the monkeys' feet, and Amba went to
    search for water
Speaking quietly with his fresh voice as he went toward
    Gorilla Lake
To all the beasts. Wan Kai lifted his body from the rice
    mat
When his brother Ten Ko came running in. "They have
    agreed in the village,"
He said. Win Tei brought them tea. Outside the rain
Fell. Plop, plop. Daisy felt something stir inside her.
She went to the window and looked out at the snow. Louis
    came up the stairs
With the milk. "Roon has bronchitis," said the American
    doctor,
"She will have to stay inside for ten days during this rain."
    Amba
Plucked a violently purple blossom from the tree. Angebor
Sneaked away, and wanted to go there again, but Maggia
    said he could not go again in this rain
And would be sure to lose the money for the *oona*. Baba
    stared
At the green and black sea. Uncle Dad stood up in the
    boat, while Baba
Watched Father plunge his harpoon three times in the
    whale. Daisy turned
Dreamily around, her hand on her cheek. Frank's boot
Kicked in the door. Amba wept; Ahna the deer was dead;
    she lay amid her puzzled young.
The sweet forms of the apple blossoms bent down to
    Wehtukai.
The boat split. Sun streamed into the apartment. Amba,
    Amba!
The lake was covered with gloom. Enna plunged into it
    screaming.

THE DEPARTURE FROM HYDRA

As I was walking home just now, from seeing
Margaret and Norris off (though Peter,
An Englishman whom Norris had met yesterday,
Went back to change his clothes, and missed the boat),
As I came home along the little street
Without a name on which the only theatre,
The movie theatre, on Hydra is,
Called "The Gardenia" or just plain "Gardenia,"
The street which they today are tearing up
And carrying new stones in to replace
The ones they're tearing up, though it may be
They are the same stones, put in different order
Or in a different way, as I was walking,
With the heat of the day just over, at five-thirty,
I felt quite good, but then felt an awareness
Of something in my legs that might be painful
And then of some slight tension in my jaws
And slight pains in my head; instead of despairing
And giving all thought of pleasure up, I felt
That if I could write down all that I felt
As I came walking there, that that would be
A pleasure also, and with solidity.
I passed a mule—some men were loading up
His fellow-mule with packets—and I stared
At his wide eyes and his long hard flat nose
Or face, at which he turned away his eyes
And stamped his right hoof nervously. I felt
Guilty, a member of a higher species
Deliberately using my power against
A natural inferior because
Really I was afraid that he might kick
When I came past; but when he seemed upset
Then I felt guilty. Then I looked ahead
And saw a view of houses on the hill,
Particularly noticing one red one
And thinking, Yes, that is a part of what
I feel, of the variety of this walk;
Then my mind blurred somewhat, I turned and came
Down this small narrow alley to my home.

As I came in, reviewing the ideas
Which had occurred to me throughout my walk,
It suddenly came to me that maybe Peter
Had missed the Athens boat deliberately;
After all, Margaret was not sure that she
Wanted to accompany him and Norris
On a walking trip on Poros, and Norris had said
He wanted to stay with Margaret, so that Peter
Was disappointed, since he and Norris had planned
That very morning to take such a walking trip,
And he, Peter, had been the most excited
Of all, about it. But now since Margaret and Norris
Were going into Athens, what was there for Peter
To do, why should he take the boat at all,
Even though he'd planned to, to stop at Poros?
Except, of course, to act on some marginal chance
That Norris might get off with him and walk,
Or on the strength of previous expectations,
Emotional impetus lingering. If not,
Perhaps his going to change was just an excuse
To avoid an actual confrontation with Norris
In which he would have to say, "No, I'm not going
Unless you'll come on the walking trip!" but he knew,
Peter, that Norris wanted to stay with Margaret
And that therefore speaking to him would only result
In a little pain and confusion, since both were quite drunk,
Having planned their trip to Poros over beer all morning;
And also, of course, it might result in his getting,
In spite of himself, on the boat, by the talk confused
And not thinking clearly (whereas if he walked away
He had only, really, to wait till the boat had left —
Then he could come back down and think it over,
Surely to find he didn't regret too much
Not getting the boat, because after all the reason
He'd wanted to take the boat had long been gone).
For a human situation often leads
People to do things that they don't desire
At all, but they find that what they did desire
Has somehow led them to this situation
In which not to do that which is proposed
Seems inconsistent, hostile, or insane,
Though much more often very unfriendly; then too
Sometimes it chiefly is a lack of time

To explain how things have changed that leads one,
   waving
One's hands, aboard a ship that bodes one ill.
To walk away as Peter did is one way
Of avoiding such situations—another way
Is never to deceive or have high hopes
For foolish things; to be straight with oneself,
With one's own body, nature, and society,
To cast off everything that is not clear
And definite, and move toward one desire
After another, with no afterthoughts.
Living in this way one avoids the sudden
Transports of excitement Peter felt
When Norris mentioned a Poros walking tour.
For surely if Peter's natural desires
Had all been satisfied, if his life were running
Smoothly sexually, and if his health
Were excellent and his work going well,
He scarcely would have gotten so excited
At the mere thought of walking around Poros;
This sort of thing, however, often happens
To people from Northern countries, not just Peter,
And perhaps if one is English, Norse, or Swedish,
Danish, Finnish, Swiss, or North American,
One cannot avoid a certain amount of tension,
A certain quavering in the hand which reaches
For a ripe peach or the shoulder of a girl,
One whom, as one walks back from going swimming,
One thinks that one could eat, she's so delicious,
But only thinks it for a little while
(This thought itself is such a Northern one!
A Southerner would think about a place
Where he could go and jump on top of her) —
In any case, then, Northerners find it hard
To avoid such sudden excitements, but the English,
And especially the upper class, are worst of all,
Because besides their climate that's oppressed them
There's also been a restrictive upbringing,
Manners around the house perhaps too severe
For children—I am speaking of those English
Who escape from "class" and become bright or artistic,
The ones one sees on places like this island
(These sudden outbursts of enthusiasm, of course,

Are often much admired by other people,
Particularly some not very smart ones,
Who think however they're very sensitive
And what they most admire is "vitality"
Which they think things like outbursts are a sign of,
And they can bore you far into the night
With telling you how wonderful some Dane
Or Norsky is, when you could be asleep
Dreaming of satisfying your desires
With persons who are always very warm,
Tender, and exciting—but, awake!
They're talking still, and though your sickly smile
Gets sicklier every moment, they go on:
"Hans suddenly got the idea to
Inundate Denmark. He is wonderful!"
"Oh, marvelous! Where does one go to meet him?"
"I'll give you his address. He has a farm
Where he stays in the summer; he loves animals,
But sometimes when he drinks a lot he beats them
And says that he can understand their language."
"How marvelous!" "And here's his city address:
Beschtungen aber Bass Gehundenweiss
996." "Goodnight." But Peter is
Not an exaggerated case like that,
And not a nagging bore who talks of such
People, but he has "outbursts" all the same.
It is true, in a sense these outbursts are
Difficult to discriminate from real
Vitality, which everyone esteems
These days because of man's oppressed position
In modern society, which saps his strength
And makes him want to do what everyone else does,
Whereas some man who says, "Let's pitch the glasses
Against the lamppost" is likely to be praised
By some low-IQ person who is there
As being really vital, ah he's wonderful.
Vitality, however, usually
Appeals to an answering vital force in others
And brings about making love or great events,
Or it at least gives pleasure—I can't judge
Vitality in any way but the way
It gives me pleasure, for if I do not get
Pleasure from life, of which vitality

Is just the liquid form, then what am I
And who cares what I say? I for one don't.
Therefore I judge vitality that way.)
But Peter, after having this idea
Of a walking trip on Poros, must have felt
That in walking around in the sun all day on an island
About which he knew nothing, there might come
Some insight to him or some relaxation,
Some feeling the way an Italian feels all the time,
Or perhaps not, perhaps he never does;
Peter at any rate was probably not
Conscious of an Italian at the time
He thought with pleasure about the walk on Poros,
But there he was, faced with Norris and Margaret
An hour before the boat came in, and Norris
Was saying "Maybe not." One mistake of Peter,
Or, rather, difficulty, a common one
In such enthusiasms, is that since
One's enthusiasm is motivated by submerged
Feelings and so its object isn't clear
To anyone, it is most likely that
Though they respond excitedly at first,
Partly because excitement is so communicable,
Others, when they think over what you've planned,
Will see it in a greyer light, unless of course
They have the same neuroses that you have,
In which case a whole lifetime might be built
Upon one of these outbursts. Norris, probably,
In drinking with Peter, wanted more than anything
To be agreeable, whereas Peter wanted
To "do" something unusual, not necessarily
Pleasing to Norris, not necessarily displeasing;
Norris, I should imagine, then, once he
Was out of Peter's company, since he'd known him
A very short time, was lacking the chief impulse
That motivated him when he agreed
To take a tour with Peter; therefore Margaret,
Speaking to Norris when he was alone
And saying she did not want to take the trip,
Found he immediately agreed with her,
Expressed some doubts at least, and said all right,
The trip was off then, he'd explain to Peter;
Peter, of course, was very surprised by this,

But still he must have been used to it because
The way that Norris and Margaret acted was based
On laws of human conduct which endure;
And since that outburst surely was not his first,
Peter was probably accustomed to
That sort of outcome of his impulses
And said to himself, "Ah, they don't understand,"
But probably knew inside that there was something
Seriously the matter with him. So when he left
The table and said, "I'm going to get my things,"
It was with a certain tension that he left,
Indicative of the fact he'd not come back,
And of the fact that he knew he would not avoid
Self-doubts because he avoided the useless boat trip;
Of course he wouldn't think he should have gone
But wonder why things had been the way they were.
It was these deeper worries in his mind,
I think, that kept him from leaving even sooner
With the same excuse, rather than a hope that Norris
Would change his mind again. Deep thoughts make
    helpless
Men for small undertakings. Well, perhaps
The last is speculation, but the rest
Seems surely true. I smiled, and closed the door.

Allen Ginsberg

KADDISH

For Naomi Ginsberg 1894 - 1956

i

Strange now to think of you, gone without corsets & eyes,
        while I walk on the sunny pavement of Greenwich
        Village.
downtown Manhattan, clear winter noon, and I've been
        up all night, talking, talking, reading the Kaddish
        aloud, listening to Ray Charles blues shout blind on
        the phonograph
the rhythm the rhythm—and your memory in my head
        three years after—And read Adonais' last
        triumphant stanzas aloud—wept, realizing how we
        suffer—
And now Death is that remedy all singers dream of, sing,
        remember, prophesy as in the Hebrew Anthem, or
        the Buddhist Book of Answers—and my own
        imagination of a withered leaf—at dawn—
Dreaming back thru life, Your time—and mine
        accelerating toward Apocalypse,
the final moment—the flower burning in the Day—and
        what comes after,
looking back on the mind itself that saw an American city
a flash away, and the great dream of Me or China, or you
        and a phantom Russia, or a crumpled bed that
        never existed—
like a poem in the dark—escaped back to Oblivion—
No more to say, and nothing to weep for but the Beings
        in the Dream, trapped in its disappearance,
sighing, screaming with it, buying and selling pieces of
        phantom, worshipping each other,
worshipping the God included in it all—longing or
        inevitability?—while it lasts, a Vision—anything
        more?
It leaps about me, as I go out and walk the street, look
        back over my shoulder, Seventh Avenue, the
        battlements of window office buildings shouldering

each other high, under a cloud, tall as the sky an
    instant—and the sky above—an old blue place.
or down the Avenue to the South, to—as I walk toward the
    Lower East Side—where you walked 50 years
    ago, little girl—from Russia, eating the first
    poisonous tomatoes of America—frightened on the
    dock—
then struggling in the crowds of Orchard Street toward
    what?—toward Newark—
toward candy store, first home-made sodas of the century,
    hand-churned ice cream in backroom on musty
    brownfloor boards—
Toward education marriage nervous breakdown,
    operation, teaching school, and learning to be mad,
    in a dream—what is this life?
Toward the Key in the window—and the great Key lays its
    head of light on top of Manhattan, and over the
    floor, and lays down on the sidewalk—in a single
    vast beam, moving, as I walk down First toward the
    Yiddish Theater—and the place of poverty
you knew, and I know, but without caring now—Strange to
    have moved thru Paterson, and the West, and
    Europe and here again,
with the cries of Spaniards now in the doorstoops doors
    and dark boys on the street, fire escapes old as you
—Tho you're not old now, that's left here with me—
Myself, anyhow, maybe as old as the universe—and I guess
    that dies with us—enough to cancel all that comes
    —What came is gone forever every time—
That's good! That leaves it open for no regret—no fear
    radiators, lacklove, torture even toothache in the
    end—
Though while it comes it is a lion that eats the soul—and
    the lamb, the soul, in us, alas, offering itself in
    sacrifice to change's fierce hunger—hair and teeth
    —and the roar of bonepain, skull bare, break rib,
    rot-skin, braintricked Implacability.
Ai! ai! we do worse! We are in a fix! And you're out, Death
    let you out, Death had the Mercy, you're done with
    your century, done with God, done with the path
    thru it—Done with yourself at last—Pure—Back
    to the Babe dark before your Father, before us all—
    before the world—

There, rest. No more suffering for you. I know where
        you've gone, it's good.
No more flowers in the summer of fields of New York, no
        joy now, no more fear of Louis,
and no more of his sweetness and glasses, his high school
        decades, debts, loves, frightened telephone calls,
        conception beds, relatives, hands—
No more of sister Elanor,—she gone before you—we kept
        it secret—you killed her—or she killed herself to bear
        with you—an arthritic heart—But Death's killed you
        both—No matter—
Nor your memory of your mother, 1915 tears in silent
        movies weeks and weeks—forgetting, agrieve
        watching Marie Dressler address humanity,
        Chaplin dance in youth,
or Boris Godinov, Chaliapin's at the Met, halling his voice
        of a weeping Czar—by standing room with Elanor
        & Max—watching also the Capitalists take seats in
        Orchestra, white furs, diamonds,
with the YPSL's hitch-hiking thru Pennsylvania, in black
        baggy gym skirts pants, photograph of 4 girls
        holding each other round the waist, and laughing
        eye, too coy, virginal solitude of 1920
all girls grown old, or dead, now, and that long hair in the
        grave—lucky to have husbands later—
You made it—I came too—Eugene my brother before
        (still grieving now and will gream on to his last
        stiff hand, as he goes thru his cancer—or kill—
        later perhaps—soon he will think—
And it's the last moment I remember, which I see them
        all, thru myself, now—tho not you
I didn't foresee what you felt—what more hideous gape of
        bad mouth came first—to you—and were you
        prepared?
To go where? In that Dark—that—in that God? a
        radiance? A Lord in the Void? Like an eye in the
        black cloud in a dream? Adonoi at last, with you?
Beyond my remembrance! Incapable to guess! Not merely
        the yellow skull in the grave, or a box of worm
        dust, and a stained ribbon—Deathshead with
        Halo? can you believe it?
Is it only the sun that shines once for the mind, only the
        flash of existence, than none ever was?

Nothing beyond what we have—what you had—that so
      pitiful—yet Triumph,
to have been here, and changed, like a tree, broken, or
      flower—fed to the ground—but mad, with its
      petals, colored, thinking Great Universe, shaken,
      cut in the head, leaf stript, hid in an egg crate
      hospital, cloth wrapped, sore—freaked in the moon
      brain, Naughtless.
No flower like that flower, which knew itself in the garden,
      and fought the knife—lost
Cut down by an idiot Snowman's icy—even in the Spring
      —strange ghost thought—some Death—Sharp
      icicle in his hand—crowned with old roses—a dog
      for his eyes—cock of a sweatshop—heart of electric
      irons.
All the accumulations of life, that wear us out—clocks,
      bodies, consciousness, shoe, breasts—begotten sons
      —your Communism—'Paranoia' into hospitals.
You once kicked Elanor in the leg, she died of heart failure
      later. You of stroke. Asleep? within a year, the two
      of you, sisters in death. Is Elanor happy?
Max grieves alive in an office on Lower Broadway, lone
      large mustache over midnight Accountings, not
      sure. His life passes—as he sees—and what does he
      doubt now? Still dreaming of making money, or
      that might have made money, hired nurse, had
      children, found even your Immortality, Naomi?
I'll see him soon. Now I've got to cut through—to talk to
      you—as I didn't when you had a mouth.
Forever. And we're bound for that, Forever—like Emily
      Dickinson's horses—headed to the End.
They know the way—These Steeds—run faster than we
      think—it's our own life they cross—and take with
      them.

    Magnificent, mourned no more, marred of heart, mind
behind, married dreamed, mortal changed—Ass and face
done with murder.
    In the world, given, flower maddened, made no
Utopia, shut under pine, almed in Earth, balmed in Lone,
Jehovah, accept.
    Nameless, One Faced, Forever beyond me,
beginningless, endless, Father in death. Tho I am not

there for this Prophecy, I am unmarried, I'm hymnless,
I'm Heavenless, headless in blisshood I would still adore

Thee, Heaven, after Death, only One blessed in
Nothingness, not light or darkness, Dayless Eternity—

Take this, this Psalm, from me, burst from my hand in
a day, some of my Time, now given to Nothing—to praise
Thee—But Death

This is the end, the redemption from Wilderness,
way for the Wonderer, House sought for All, black
handkerchief washed clean by weeping—page beyond
Psalm—Last change of mine and Naomi—to God's perfect
Darkness—Death, stay thy phantoms!

ii

Over and over—refrain—of the Hospitals—still haven't
written your history—leave it abstract—a few images

run thru the mind—like the saxophone chorus of
houses and years—remembrance of electrical shocks.

By long nites as a child in Paterson apartment,
watching over your nervousness—you were fat—your next
move—

By that afternoon I stayed home from school to take
care of you—once and for all—when I vowed forever that
once man disagreed with my opinion of the cosmos, I was
lost—

But my later burden—vow to illuminate mankind—
this is release of particulars—(mad as you)—(sanity a
trick of agreement)—

But you stared out the window on the Broadway
Church corner, and spied a mystical assassin from Newark,

So phoned the Doctor—'OK go way for a rest'—so I
put on my coat and walked you downstreet—On the way a
grammarschool boy screamed, unaccountably—'Where
you goin Lady to Death'? I shuddered—

and you covered your nose with motheaten fur
collar, gas mask against poison sneaked into downtown
atmosphere, sprayed by Grandma—

And was the driver of the cheesebox Public Service bus
a member of the gang? You shuddered at his face, I could
hardly get you on—to New York, very Times Square, to
grab another Greyhound—

where we hung around 2 hours fighting invisible bugs
and jewish sickness—breeze poisoned by Roosevelt—

out to get you—and me tagging along, hoping it would end in a quiet room in a victorian house by a lake.

Ride 3 hours thru tunnels past all American industry, Bayonne preparing for World War II, tanks, gas fields, soda factories, diners, locomotive roundhouse fortress—into piney woods New Jersey Indians—calm towns—long roads thru sandy tree fields—

Bridges by deerless creeks, old wampum loading the streambed—down there a tomahawk or Pocahontas bone —and a million old ladies voting for Roosevelt in brown small houses, roads off the Madness Highway—

perhaps a hawk in a tree, or a hermit looking for an owl-filled branch—

All the time arguing—afraid of strangers in the forward double set, snoring regardless—what busride they snore on now?

'Allen, you don't understand—it's—ever since those 3 big sticks up my back—they did something to me in Hospital, they poisoned me, they want to see me dead— 3 big sticks, 3 big sticks—

"The Bitch! Old Grandma! Last week I saw her, dressed in pants like an old man, with a sack on her back, climbing up the brick side of the apartment

'On the fire escape, with poison germs, to throw on me —at night—maybe Louis is helping her—he's under her power—

'I'm your mother, take me to Lakewood' (near where Graf Zeppelin had crashed before, all Hitler in Explosion) 'where I can hide.'

We got there—Dr. Whatzis rest home—she hid behind a closet—demanded a blood transfusion.

We were kicked out—tramping with Valise to unknown shady lawn houses—dusk, pine trees after dark —long dead street filled with crickets and poison ivy—

I shut her up by now—big house REST HOME ROOMS—gave the landlady her money for the week— carried up the iron valise—sat on bed waiting to escape—

Neat room in attic with friendly bedcover—lace curtains—spinning wheel rug—Stained wallpaper old as Naomi. We were home.

I left on the next bus to New York—lay my head back in the last seat, depressed—the worst yet to come?— abandoning her, rode in torpor—I was only 12.

Would she hide in her room and come out cheerful for breakfast? Or lock her door and stare thru the window for sidestreet spies? Listen at keyholes for Hitlerian invisible gas? Dream in a chair—or mock me, by—in front of a mirror, alone?

12 riding the bus at nite thru New Jersey, have left Naomi to Parcae in Lakewood's haunted house—left to my own fate bus—sunk in a seat—all violins broken—my heart sore in my ribs—mind was empty—Would she were safe in her coffin—

Or back at Normal School in Newark, studying up on American in a black skirt—winter on the street without lunch—a penny a pickle—home at night to take care of Elanor in the bedroom—

First nervous breakdown was 1919—she stayed home from school and lay in a dark room for three weeks— something bad—never said what—every noise hurt— dreams of the creaks of Wall Street—

Before the grey Depression—went upstate New York —recovered—Lou took photo of her sitting crossleg on the grass—her long hair wound with flowers—smiling— playing lullabies on mandolin—poison ivy smoke in left-wing summer camps and me in infancy saw trees—

or back teaching school, laughing with idiots, the backward classes—her Russian specialty—morons with dreamy lips, great eyes, thin feet & sicky fingers, swaybacked, rachitic—

great heads pendulous over Alice in Wonderland, a blackboard full of C A T.

Naomi reading patiently, story out of a Communist fairy book—Tale of the Sudden Sweetness of The Dictator —Forgiveness of Warlocks—Armies Kissing—

Deathsheads Around the Green Table—The King & the Workers—Paterson Press printed them up in the 30's till she went mad, or they folded, both.

O Paterson! I got home late that nite. Louis was worried. How could I be so—didn't I think? I shouldn't have left her. Mad in Lakewood. Call the Doctor. Phone the home in the pines. Too late.

Went to bed exhausted, wanting to leave the world (probably that year newly in love with R—my high school mind hero, jewish boy who came a doctor later—then silent neat kid—

I later laying down life for him, moved to Manhattan
—followed him to college—Prayed on ferry to help
mankind if admitted—vowed, the day I journeyed to
Entrance Exam—

by being honest revolutionary labor lawyer—would
train for that—inspired by Sacco Vanzetti, Norman
Thomas, Debs, Altgeld, Sandburg, Poe—Little Blue
Books. I wanted to be President, or Senator.

ignorant woe—later dreams of kneeling by R's shocked
knees declaring my love of 1941—What sweetness he'd
have shown me, tho, that I'd wished him & despaired—
first love—a crush—

Later a mortal avalanche, whole mountains of
homosexuality, Matterhorns of cock, Grand Canyons of
asshole—weight on my melancholy head—

meanwhile I walked on Broadway imagining Infinity
like a rubber ball without space beyond—what's outside?
—coming home to Graham Avenue still melancholy
passing the lone green hedges across the street, dreaming
after the movies—)

The telephone rang at 2 A.M.—Emergency—she'd gone
mad—Naomi hiding under the bed screaming bugs of
Mussolini—Help! Louis! Buba! Fascists! Death!—the
landlady frightened—old fag attendant screaming back at
her—

Terror, that woke the neighbors—old ladies on the
second floor recovering from menopause—all those rags
between thighs, clean sheets, sorry over lost babies—
husbands ashen—children sneering at Yale, or putting oil
in hair at CCNY—or trembling in Montclair State
Teachers College like Eugene—

Her big leg crouched to her breast, hand outstretched
Keep Away, wool dress on her thighs, fur coat dragged
under the bed—she barricaded herself under bedspring
with suitcases.

Louis in pyjamas listening to phone, frightened—do
now?—Who could know?—my fault, delivering her to
solitude?—sitting in the dark room on the sofa, trembling,
to figure out—

He took the morning train to Lakewood, Naomi still
under bed—thought he brought poison Cops—Naomi
screaming—Louis what happened to your heart then?
Have you been killed by Naomi's ecstasy?

Dragged her out, around the corner, a cab, forced her in with valise, but the driver left them off at drugstore. Bus stop, two hours wait.

I lay in bed nervous in the 4-room apartment, the big bed in living room, next to Louis' desk—shaking—he came home that nite, late, told me what happened.

Naomi at the prescription counter defending herself from the enemy—racks of children's books, douche bags, aspirins, pots, blood—'Don't come near me—murderers! Keep away! Promise not to kill me!'

Louis in horror at the soda fountain—with Lakewood girlscouts—coke addicts—nurses—busmen hung on schedule—Police from country precinct, dumbed—and a priest dreaming of pigs on an ancient cliff?

Smelling the air—Louis pointing to emptiness?— Customers vomiting their cokes—or staring—Louis humiliated—Naomi trimphant—The Announcement of the Plot. Bus arrives, the drivers won't have them on trip to New York.

Phonecalls to Dr. Whatzis, 'She needs a rest,' The mental hospital—State Greystone Doctors—'Bring her here, Mr. Ginsberg.'

Naomi, Naomi—sweating, bulge-eyed, fat, the dress unbuttoned at one side—hair over brow, her stocking hanging evilly on her legs—screaming for a blood transfusion—one righteous hand upraised—a shoe in it— barefoot in the Pharmacy—

The enemies approach—what poisons? Tape recorders? FBI? Zhdanov hiding behind the counter? Trotsky mixing rat bacteria in the back of the store? Uncle Sam in Newark, plotting deathly perfumes in the Negro district? Uncle Ephraim, drunk with murder in the politician's bar, scheming of Hague? Aunt Rose passing water thru the needles of the Spanish Civil War?

till the hired $35 ambulance came from Red Bank— —Grabbed her arms—strapped her on the stretcher— moaning, poisoned by imaginaries, vomiting chemicals thru Jersey, begging mercy from Essex County to Morristown—

And back to Greystone where she lay three years— that was the last breakthrough, delivered her to Madhouse again—

On what wards—I walked there later, oft—old

catatonic ladies, grey as cloud or ash or walls—sit crooning over floorspace—Chairs—and the wrinkled hags acreep, accusing—begging my 13-year-old mercy—

'Take me home'—I went alone sometimes looking for the lost Naomi, taking Shock—and I'd say, 'No, you're crazy Mama,—Trust the Drs.'—

And Eugene, my brother, her elder son, away studying Law in a furnished room in Newark—

came Paterson-ward next day—and he sat on the broken-down couch in the living room—'We had to send her back to Greystone'—

—his face perplexed, so young, then eyes with tears— then crept weeping all over his face—'What for?' wail vibrating in his cheekbones, eyes closed up, high voice— Eugene's face of pain.

Him faraway, escaped to an Elevator in the Newark Library, his bottle daily milk on windowsill of $5 week furn room downtown at trolley tracks—

He worked 8 hrs. a day for $20/wk—thru Law School years—stayed by himself innocent near negro whorehouses.

Unlaid, poor virgin—writing poems about Ideals and politics letters to the editor Pat Eve News—(we both wrote, denouncing Senator Borah and Isolationists—and felt mysterious toward Paterson City Hall—

I sneaked inside it once—local Moloch tower with phallus spire & cap o' ornament, strange gothic Poetry that stood on Market Street—replica Lyons' Hotel de Ville—

wings, balcony & scrollwork portals, gateway to the giant city clock, secret map room full of Hawthorne— dark Debs in the Board of Tax—Rembrandt smoking in the gloom—

Silent polished desks in the great committee room— Aldermen? Bd of Finance? Mosca the hairdresser aplot— Crapp the gangster issuing orders from the john—The madmen struggling over Zone, Fire, Cops & Backroom Metaphysics—we're all dead—outside by the bus-stop Eugene stared thru childhood—

where the Evangelist preached madly for 3 decades, hard-haired, cracked & true to his mean Bible—chalked Prepare to Meet Thy God on civic pave—

or God is Love on the railroad overpass concrete—he

raved like I would rave, the lone Evangelist—Death on City Hall—)

But Gene, young,—been Montclair Teachers College 4 years—taught half year & quit to go ahead in life—afraid of Discipline Problems—dark sex Italian students, raw girls getting laid, no English, sonnets disregarded—and he did not know much—just that he lost—

so broke his life in two and paid for Law—read huge blue books and rode the ancient elevator 13 miles away in Newark & studied up hard for the future.

just found the Scream of Naomi on his failure doorstep, for the final time, Naomi gone, us lonely—home —him sitting there—

Then have some chicken soup, Eugene. The Man of Evangel wails in front of City Hall. And this year Lou has poetic loves of suburb middle-age—in secret—music from his 1937 book—Sincere—he longs for beauty—

No love since Naomi screamed—since 1923?—now lost in Greystone ward—new shock for her—Electricity, following the 40 Insulin.

And Metrasol had made her fat.

So that a few years later she came home again—we'd much advanced and planned—I waited for that day—my Mother again to cook &—play the piano—sing at mandoline—Lung Stew, & Stenka Razin, & the communist line on the war with Finland—and Louis in debt—suspected to be poisoned money—mysterious capitalisms

—& walked down the long front hall & looked at the furniture. She never remembered it all. Some amnesia. Examined the doilies—and the dining room set was sold—

the Mahogany table—20 years love—gone to the junk man—we still had the piano—and the book of Poe—and the Mandolin, tho needed some string, dusty—

She went to the backroom to lay down in bed and ruminate, a nap, hide—I went in with her, not leave her by herself—lay in bed next to her—shades pulled, dusky, late afternoon—Louis in front room at desk, waiting—perhaps boiling chicken for supper—

'Don't be afraid of me because I'm just coming back home from the mental hospital—I'm your mother—'

Poor love, lost—a fear—I lay there—Said, 'I love you

Naomi,'—stiff, next to her arm. I would have cried, was this the comfortless lone union?—Nervous, and she got up soon.

Was she ever satisfied? And—by herself sat on the new couch by the front windows, uneasy—cheek leaning on her hand—narrowing eye—at what fate that day—

Picking her tooth with her nail, lips formed an O, suspicion—thought's old worn vagina—absent sideglance of eye—some evil debt written in the wall, unpaid—& the aged breasts of Newark come near—

May have heard radio gossip thru the wires in her head, controlled by 3 big sticks left in her back by gangsters in amnesia, thru the hospital—caused pain between her shoulders)—

Into her head—Roosevelt should know her case, she told me—Afraid to kill her, now, that the government knew their names—traced back to Hitler—wanted to leave Louis' house forever.

One night, sudden attack—her noise in the bathroom— like croaking up her soul—convulsions and red vomit coming out of her mouth—diarrhea water exploding from her behind—on all fours in front of the toilet—urine running between her legs—left retching on the tile floor smeared with her black feces—unfainted—

At forty, varicosed, nude, fat, doomed, hiding outside the apartment door near the elevator calling Police, yelling for her girl-friend Rose to help—

Once locked herself in with razor or iodine—could hear her cough in tears at sink—Lou broke through glass green-painted door, we pulled her out to the bedroom.

Then quiet for months that winter—walks, alone, nearby on Broadway, read Daily Worker—Broke her arm, fell on icy street—

Began to scheme escape from cosmic financial murder plots—later she ran away to the Bronx to her sister Elanor. And there's another saga of late Naomi in New York.

Or thru Elanor or the Workman's Circle, where she worked, addressing envelopes, she made out—went shopping for Campbell's tomato soup—saved money Louis mailed her—

Later she found a boyfriend, and he was a doctor—Dr. Isaac worked for National Maritime Union—now Italian

bald and pudgy old doll—who was himself an orphan—
but they kicked him out—Old cruelties—

Sloppier, sat around on bed or chair, in corset dreaming
to herself—'I'm hot—I'm getting fat—I used to have such
a beautiful figure before I went to the hospital—You
should have seen me in Woodbine—' This in a furnished
room around the NMU hall, 1943.

Looking at naked baby pictures in the magazine—baby
powder advertisements, strained lamb carrots—'I will
think nothing but beautiful thoughts.'

Revolving her head round and round on her neck at
window light in summertime, in hypnotize, in doven-
dream recall—

'I touch his cheek, I touch his cheek, he touches my
lips with his hand, I think beautiful thoughts, the baby
has a beautiful hand.'—

Or a No-shake of her body, disgust—some thought of
Buchenwald—some insulin passes thru her head—a
grimace nerve shudder at Involuntary (as shudder when I
piss)—bad chemical in her cortex—'No don't think of
that. He's a rat.'

Naomi: 'And when we die we become an onion, a
cabbage, a carrot, or a squash, a vegetable.' I come
downtown from Columbia and agree. She reads the Bible,
thinks beautiful thoughts all day.

'Yesterday I saw God. What did he look like? Well, in
the afternoon I climbed up a ladder—he has a cheap
cabin in the country, like Monroe, NY the chicken farms
in the wood. He was a lonely old man with a white beard.

'I cooked supper for him. I made him a nice supper—
lentil soup, vegetables, bread & butter—miltz—he sat
down at the table and ate, he was sad.

'I told him, Look at all those fightings and killings down
there, What's the matter? Why don't you put a stop to it?

'I try, he said—That's all he could do, he looked tired.
He's a bachelor so long, and he likes lentil soup.'

Serving me meanwhile, a plate of cold fish—chopped
raw cabbage dript with tapwater—smelly tomatoes—
week-old health food—grated beets & carrots with leaky
juice, warm—more and more disconsolate food—I can't
eat it for nausea sometimes—the Charity of her hands
stinking with Manhattan, madness, desire to please me,
cold undercooked fish—pale red near the bones. Her

smells—and oft naked in the room, so that I stare ahead, or turn a book ignoring her.

One time I thought she was trying to make me come lay her—flirting to herself at sink—lay back on huge bed that filled most of the room, dress up round her hips, big slash of hair, scars of operations, pancreas, belly wounds, abortions, appendix, stitching of incisions pulling down in the fat like like hideous thick zippers—ragged long lips between her legs—What, even, smell of asshole? I was cold—later revolted a little, not much—seemed perhaps a good idea to try—know the Monster of the Beginning Womb—Perhaps—that way. Would she care? She needs a lover.

Yisborach, v'yistabach, v'yispoar, v'yisroman, v'yisnaseh, v'yishador, v'yishalleh, v'hishallol, sh'meh d'kudsho, b'rich hu.

And Louis reestablishing himself in Paterson grimy apartment in negro district—living in dark rooms—but found himself a girl he later married, falling in love again —tho sere & shy—hurt with 20 years Naomi's mad idealism.

Once I came home, after longtime in N.Y., he's lonely —sitting in the bedroom, he at desk chair turned round to face me—weeps, tears in red eyes under his glasses—

That we'd left him—Gene gone strangely into army— she out on her own in NY, almost childish in her furnished room. So Louis walked downtown to postoffice to get mail, taught in highschool—stayed at poetry desk, forlorn—ate grief at Bickford's all these years—are gone.

Eugene got out of the Army, came home changed and lone—cut off his nose in jewish operation—for years stopped girls on Broadway for cups of coffee to get laid— Went to NYU, serious there, to finish Law.—

And Gene lived with her, ate naked fishcakes, cheap, while she got crazier—He got thin, or felt helpless, Naomi striking 1920 poses at the moon, half-naked in the next bed.

bit his nails and studied—was the weird nurse-son— Next year he moved to a room near Columbia—though she wanted to live with her children—

'Listen to your mother's plea, I beg you'—Louis still sending her checks—I was in bughouse that year 8 months —my own visions unmentioned in this here Lament—

But then went half mad—Hitler in her room, she saw

his mustache in the sink—afraid of Dr. Isaac now, suspecting that he was in on the Newark plot—went up to Bronx to live near Elanor's Rheumatic Heart—

And Uncle Max never got up before noon, tho Naomi at 6 A.M. was listening to the radio for spies—or searching the windowsill,

for in the empty lot downstairs, an old man creeps with his bag stuffing packages of garbage in his hanging black overcoat.

Max's sister Edie works—17 years bookkeeper at Gimbels—lived downstairs in apartment house, divorced— so Edie took in Naomi on Rochambeau Ave—

Woodlawn Cemetery across the street, vast dale of graves where Poe once—Last stop on Bronx subway—lots of communists in that area.

Who enrolled for painting classes at night in Bronx Adult High School—walked alone under Van Cortlandt Elevated line to class—paints Naomiisms—

Humans sitting on the grass in some Camp No-Worry summers yore—saints with droopy faces and long-ill-fitting pants, from hospital—

Brides in front of Lower East Side with short grooms —lost El trains running over the Babylonian apartment rooftops in the Bronx—

Sad paintings—but she expressed herself. Her mando-lin gone, all strings broke in her head, she tried. Toward Beauty? or some old life Message?

But started kicking Elanor, and Elanor had heart trouble—came upstairs and asked her about Spydom for hours,—Elanor frazzled. Max away at office, accounting for cigar stores till at night.

'I am a great woman—am truly a beautiful soul—and because of that they (Hitler, Grandma, Hearst, the Capitalists, Franco, Daily News, the 20's, Mussolini, the living dead) want to shut me up—Buba's the head of a spider network—'

Kicking the girls, Edie & Elanor—Woke Edie at midnite to tell her she was a spy and Elanor a rat. Edie worked all day and couldn't take it—She was organizing the union.—And Elanor began dying, upstairs in bed.

The relatives call me up, she's getting worse—I was the only one left—Went on the subway with Eugene to see her, ate stale fish—

'My sister whispers in the radio—Louis must be in the

apartment—his mother tells him what to say—LIARS!—I cooked for my two children—I played the mandolin—'

Last night the nightingale woke me/Last night when all was still/it sang in the golden moonlight/from on the wintry hill. She did.

I pushed her against the door and shouted 'DON'T KICK ELANOR!'—she stared at me—Contempt—die—disbelief her sons are so naïve, so dumb—'Elanor is the worst spy! She's taking orders!'

'—No wires in the room!'—I'm yelling at her—last ditch, Eugene listening on the bed—what can he do to escape that fatal Mama—'You've been away from Louis years already—Grandma's too old to walk—'

We're all alive at once then—even me & Gene & Naomi in one mythological Cousinesque room—screaming at each other in the Forever—I in Columbia jacket, she half undressed.

I banging against her head which she saw Radios, Sticks, Hitlers—the gamut of Hallucinations—for real—her own universe—no road that goes elsewhere—to my own—No America, not even a world—

That you go as all men, as Van Gogh, as mad Hannah, all the same—to the last doom—Thunder, Spirits, Lightning!

I've seen your grave! O strange Naomi! My own—cracked grave! Shema Y'Israel—I am Svul Avrum—you—in death?

Your last night in the darkness of the Bronx—I phone-called—thru hospital to secret police

That came, when you and I were alone, shrieking at Elanor in my ear—who breathed hard in her own bed, got thin—

Nor will forget, the doorknock, at your fright of spies, —Law advancing, on my honor—Eternity entering the room—you running to the bathroom undressed, hiding in protest from the last heroic fate—

staring at my eyes, betrayed—the final cops of madness rescuing me—from your foot against the broken heart of Elanor,

your voice at Edie weary of Gimbels coming home to broken radio—and Louis needing a poor divorce, he wants to get married soon—Eugene dreaming, hiding at 125 St., suing negros for money on crud furniture, defending black girls—

Protests from the bathroom—Said you were sane— dressing in a cotton robe, your shoes, then new, your purse and newspaper clippings—no—your honesty—

as you vainly made your lips more real with lipstick, looking in the mirror to see if the Insanity was Me or a carful of police

or Grandma spying at 78—Your vision—Her climbing over the walls of the cemetery with political kidnapper's bag—or what you saw on the walls of the Bronx, in pink nightgown at midnight, staring out the window on the empty lot—

Ah Rochambeau Ave—Playground of Phantoms—last apartment in the Bronx for spies—last home for Elanor or Naomi, here these communist sisters lost their revolution—

'All right—put on your coat Mrs.—let's go—We have the wagon downstairs—you want to come with her to the station?'

The ride then—held Naomi's hand, and held her head to my breast, I'm taller—kissed her and said I did it for the best—Elanor sick—and Max with heart condition— Needs—

To me—'Why did you do this?'—'Yes Mrs., your son will have to leave you in an hour'—The Ambulance

came in a few hours—drove off at 4 A.M. to some Bellevue in the night downtown—gone to the hospital forever. I saw her led away—she waved, tears in her eyes.

Two years, after a trip to Mexico—bleak in the flat plain near Brentwood, scrub brush and grass around the unused RR train track to the crazyhouse—

new brick 20 story central building—lost on the vast lawns of madtown on Long Island—huge cities of the moon.

Asylum spreads out giant wings above the path to a minute black hole—the door—entrance thru crotch—

I went in—smelt funny—the halls again—up elevator —to a glass door on a Woman's Ward—to Naomi—Two nurses buxom white—They led her out, Naomi stared— and I gaspt—She'd had a stroke—

Too thin, shrunk on her bones—age come to Naomi—

now broken into white hair—loose dress on her skeleton—
face sunk, old! withered—cheek of crone—

One hand stiff—heaviness of forties & menopause
reduced by one heart stroke, lame now—wrinkles—a scar
on her head, the lobotomy—ruin, the hand dipping
downwards to death—

O Russian faced, woman on the grass, your long black
hair is crowned with flowers, the mandolin is on your
knees—

Communist beauty, sit here married in the summer
among daisies, promised happiness at hand—

holy mother, now you smile on your love, your world
is born anew, children run naked in the field spotted with
dandelions,

they eat in the plum tree grove at the end of the
meadow and find a cabin where a white-haired negro
teaches the mystery of his rainbarrel—

blessed daughter come to America, I long to hear your
voice again, remembering your mother's music, in the Song
of the Natural Front—

O glorious muse that bore me from the womb, gave
such first mystic life & taught me talk and music, from
whose pained head I first took Vision—

Tortured and beaten in the skull—What mad
hallucinations of the damned that drive me out of my own
skull to seek Eternity till I find Peace for Thee, O Poetry—
and for all humankind call on the Origin,

Death which is the mother of the universe!—Now
wear your nakedness forever, white flowers in your hair,
your marriage sealed behind the sky—no revolution might
destroy that maidenhood—

O beautiful Garbo of my Karma—all photographs
from 1920 in Camp Nicht-Gedeiget here unchanged—
with all the teachers from Newark—Nor Elanor be gone,
nor Max await his specter—nor Louis retire from this High
School—

Back! You! Naomi! Skull on you! Gaunt immortality
and revolution come—small broken woman—the ashen
indoor eyes of hospitals, ward greyness on skin—

'Are you a spy?' I sat at the sour table, eyes filling with
tears—'Who are you? Did Louis send you?—The wires—'

in her hair, as she beat on her head—'I'm not a bad

girl—don't murder me!—I hear the ceiling—I raised two
children—'

Two years since I'd been there—I started to cry—She
stared—nurse broke up the meeting a moment—I went
into the bathroom to hide, against the toilet white walls

'The Horror' I weeping—to see her again—'The
Horror'—as if she were dead thru funeral rot in—'The
Horror!'

I came back she yelled more—they led her away—
'You're not Allen—' I watched her her face—but she
passed by me, not looking—

Opened the door to the ward,—she went thru without
a glance back, quiet suddenly—I stared out—she looked
old—the verge of the grave—'All the Horror!'

Another year, I left NY—on West Coast in Berkeley
cottage dreamed of her soul—that, thru life, in what form
it stood in that body, ashen or manic, gone beyond joy—

near its death—with eyes—was my own love in its
form, the Naomi, my mother on earth still—sent her long
letter—& wrote hymns to the mad—Work of the merciful
Lord of Poetry

that causes the broken grass to be green, or the rock to
break in grass—or the Sun to be constant to earth—Sun
of all sunflowers and days on bright iron bridges—what
shines on old hospitals—as on my yard—

Returning from San Francisco one night, Orlovsky in
my room—Whalen in his peaceful chair—a telegram from
Gene, Naomi dead—

Outside I bent my head to the ground under the
bushes near the garage—knew she was better—

at last—not left to look on Earth alone—2 years of
solitude—no one, at age nearing 60—old woman of skulls
—once long-tressed Naomi of Bible—

or Ruth who wept in America—Rebecca aged in
Newark—David remembering his Harp, now lawyer at
Yale

or Svul Avrum—Israel Abraham—myself—to sing in
the wilderness toward God—O Elohim!—so to the end—
2 days after her death I got her letter—

Strange Prophecies anew! She wrote—'The key is in
the window, the key is in the sunlight at the window—I

have the key—Get married Allen don't take drugs—the
key is in the bars, in the sunlight in the window.
                                        Love,
                                          your mother'
        which is Naomi—

                    HYMMNN

In the world which He has created according to his will
        Blessed Praised
Magnified Lauded Exalted the Name of the Holy One
        Blessed is He!
In the house in Newark Blessed is He! In the madhouse
        Blessed is He! In the house of Death Blessed is He!
Blessed be He in homosexuality! Blessed be He in
        Paranoia! Blessed be He in the city! Blessed be He
        in the Book!
Blessed be He who dwells in the shadow! Blessed be He!
        Blessed be He!
Blessed be you Naomi in tears! Blessed be you Naomi in
        fears! Blessed Blessed Blessed in sickness!
Blessed be you Naomi in Hospitals! Blessed be you Naomi
        in Solitude! Blest be your triumph! Blest be your
        bars! Blest be your last years' loneliness!
Blest be your failure! Blest be your stroke! Blest be the
        close of your eye! Blest be the gaunt of your cheek!
        Blest be your withered thighs!
Blessed be Thee Naomi in Death! Blessed be Death!
        Blessed be Death!
Blessed be He Who leads all sorrow to Heaven! Blessed be
        He in the end!
Blessed be He who builds Heaven in Darkness! Blessed
        Blessed Blessed be He! Blessed be He! Blessed be
        Death on us All!

iii

Only to have not forgotten the beginning in which she
        drank cheap sodas in the morgues of Newark,
only to have seen her weeping on grey tables in long wards
        of her universe
only to have known the weird ideas of Hitler at the door,
        the wires in her head, the three big sticks

rammed down her back, the voices in the ceiling shrieking
out her ugly early lays for 30 years,
only to have seen the time-jumps, memory lapse, the crash
of wars, the roar and silence of a vast electric shock,
only to have seen her painting crude pictures of Elevateds
running over the rooftops of the Bronx
her brothers dead in Riverside or Russia, her lone in Long
Island writing a lost letter—and her image in the
sunlight at the window
'The key is in the sunlight at the window in the bars the
key is in the sunlight,'
only to have come to that dark night on iron bed by stroke
when the sun gone down on Long Island
and the vast Atlantic roars outside the great call of Being
to its own
to come back out of the Nightmare—divided creation—
with her head lain on a pillow of the hospital to die
—in one last glimpse—all Earth one everlasting Light in
the familiar blackout—no tears for this vision—
But that the key should be left behind—at the window—
the key in the sunlight—to the living—that can
take
that slice of light in hand—and turn the door—and look
back see
Creation glistening backwards to the same grave, size of
universe,
size of the tick of the hospital's clock on the archway over
the white door—

iv

O mother
what have I left out
O mother
what have I forgotten
O mother
farewell
with a long black shoe
farewell
with Communist Party and a broken stocking
farewell
with six dark hairs on the wen of your breast
farewell

with your old dress and a long black beard around the
     vagina
farewell
with your sagging belly
with your fear of Hitler
with your mouth of bad short stories
with your fingers of rotten mandolines
with your arms of fat Paterson porches
with your belly of strikes and smokestacks
with your chin of Trotsky and the Spanish War
with your voice singing for the decaying overbroken
     workers
with your nose of bad lay with your nose of the smell
     of the pickles of Newark
with your eyes
with your eyes of Russia
with your eyes of no money
with your eyes of false China
with your eyes of Aunt Elanor
with your eyes of starving India
with your eyes pissing in the park
with your eyes of America taking a fall
with your eyes of your failure at the piano
with your eyes of your relatives in California
with your eyes of Ma Rainey dying in an ambulance
with your eyes of Czechoslovakia attacked by robots
with your eyes going to painting class at night in the Bronx
with your eyes of the killer Grandma you see on the
     horizon from the Fire-Escape
with your eyes running naked out of the apartment
     screaming into the hall
with your eyes being led away by policemen to an
     ambulance
with your eyes strapped down on the operating table
with your eyes with the pancreas removed
with your eyes of appendix operation
with your eyes of abortion
with your eyes of ovaries removed
with your eyes of shock
with your eyes of lobotomy
with your eyes of divorce
with your eyes of stroke
with your eyes alone

with your eyes
with your eyes
with your Death full of Flowers

v

Caw caw caw crows shriek in the white sun over grave
        stones in Long Island
Lord Lord Lord Naomi underneath this grass my halflife
        and my own as hers
caw caw my eye be buried in the same Ground where I
        stand in Angel
Lord Lord great Eye that stares on All and moves in a
        black cloud
caw caw strange cry of Beings flung up into sky over the
        waving trees
Lord Lord O Grinder of giant Beyonds my voice in a
        boundless field in Sheol
Caw caw the call of Time rent out of foot and wing an
        instant in the universe
Lord Lord an echo in the sky the wind through ragged
        leaves the roar of memory
caw caw all years my birth a dream caw caw New York the
        bus the broken shoe the vast highschool caw caw
        all Visions of the Lord
Lord Lord Lord caw caw caw Lord Lord Lord caw caw caw
        Lord

N Y 1959

Jascha Kessler

REQUIEM FOR AN ABSTRACT ARTIST

*Jackson Pollock, dead August 1956,
at the wheel of his convertible.*

No world but this for your eye:
   space without nebulae, comets,
  neither cosmic dusts, stars, gas, debris,
nor, nearer, planets, sun, moon, cloud, hill, plain,
trees, birds—nothing inhuman to stir pain
  and make us love what eyes learned to see
    when forepaws left their rude comments
     on things, saying *X was I*.

No world but this in your space:
   where all is free, where Being's forms,
  born of human force, live from your act
of grace in spectrums unknown to God's white,
thrive in space like souls passing time when light
  strikes fractured glass, sand, paint smeared and tracked
    by palette knife—such random storms
     whirled over your human face

    as never racked God's creatures.
   Who can commit you then to God
  when all things are His but yours, Jackson,
who to say, "Sandy cemetery clay
holds this broken drunken artist whose play
  was work, work splash of bitter lakes on
    silent unsized canvas where good
     and bad never have features

    as in God's world of moral things,
   God's numbers not at last nameless,
  sexual, violent, or skillful
as you were in those desperate movements
of your times at work, at play, those moments
  bourbon, breasts, brush made living artful
    and so self-willed, dying aimless
     and unmindful of God's real things?"

Won't someone ask, when flowers
 dropped by Kline, de Kooning, pale wife
and fifty ranking abstract friends wilt
on your new grave and funeral turns wake,
wake floats toward next weekend, when for your sake
 flesh becomes void again, denied, killed
  for love of something in this life
   called art, "Are all man's hours

   zeroed like yours in God's eye
  and ours in yours, Jackson, useless
 colored space minus natural line,
naked spirit's elaborate gestures
knowing nothing in truth but these vestures
 of itself in its own masculine,
  own feminine, with no address
   but this home in time, this I?"

FOLLOWING THE SUN

You said, "How strange! Among all who have come by,
only you guessed my name." Hardly. I could not have
done otherwise. And now, what is mine?

No matter where it fell, the seed must do its best to become its unknown self. If you believed morality necessary too, consider the agony of the plant: its only life,
desire.

That permanent diet they forced on us—how young we
were! Some warm room, food enough, a few cigarettes,
and everywhere in our thoughts those loudspeaking communities instructing us. By such dry passions they obli-
gated us to persist, despite everything, in the one direction: towards life.

Thronged streets, people whispering "What, What?" Pale
swaths of filmy radiance, ivory, pink, chartreuse, ozone
blue, sweeping overhead though not dimming the stars:
the northern lights! Before dawn a total eclipse of the
sun, calculated how many scores of years ago, would

surely begin, eastward over the Atlantic. The great age
must be near. We waited, heroic as lampposts. Clocks
ticked loudly, then softer again: sighs of married sleepers.
Also, through the short, hot night, here and there the
thrilling noise of shattered glass—windows, bottles. Barriers and containers. That perpetual sedentary economy!
Well, but if you cared you could manage for a few years,
living together like a family. Yet when it came, on whom
would the sun shine? Oh my dear hope, how frightened
you are.

As for thought—plunged like an aging actress in her bar-
bituric pool. Darkness, and talk was misery; it filled the
ashtrays. In a while, the tide at full, men would be con-
centrating on charts held unrolled beneath the sufficient
glow of their binnacles. Business and pleasure: always
somewhere to go and a way to get there. Yet, as though
hopelessly, we brewed another pot of coffee. You could
almost feel the waters start on ebb. We knew what was
happening to us: it is never the first time for those who
remember their birth.

You were taught one of the histories, and so you take the
huge vagary of the present for granted. My faith in nothing, not even in what I do (my show of life!) makes you
anxious. You wish me to possess you, just as you need to
possess me. Often enough you even survey and dig into
tomorrow: you suppose that buying an old well-built
house and moving it to your own new foundation where
you can overlook this dairygreen valley in which farmers
fought side by side with Indians will bring us America.
All right, then what? You'll only see me there, mowing
the lawn again. Maybe I stop, go to the ragged screen of
privet to peer through. Maybe I've glimpsed the shadow
of implicit ruin moving once more in Mr. Wester's tall
August hay, careless as the black bear who slouched
through the sumac at the bottom of the meadow. A
tremor. Maybe you will remember, dear, what a surprise
our meeting was, too. Springs flowing in one eon, in another not . . .

One need only want to join those who have imagined a
true change of seasons to understand that space and time

exist, and yet do not. For each of the few thousand miles which separate those brief life expectancies of lovers they have prepared a fear, each fear a thought that stops them, and stopping, they contemplate the killing distances that lie beyond the next step. The first piece of gravel I pick up from my driveway reveals a fossil snail!

But we have no destiny at all! This planet spins on, fixed in a lucky orbit. The single stars themselves, which we resolve as clusters of random, dimming universes, drift nowhere. Dreading your reply, I said, "Where do you want to go?" It was what I expected, the only one: "With you."

As long as the car was moving, whatever we said made sense. And whenever we stopped for the night it seemed useless to utter anything but the common syllable of endearments.

Day and night, the diesels of the combines roaring. Cutting, husking, threshing, baling, bagging, loading, they disappear over the flat bluegray horizon, following their compasses north-by-northwest. High summer. The spume of their exhausts, grayblue, tinges the haze. Up in the sky swifts and swallows careen; redwinged blackbirds tilt on the fenceposts; crows cross cawing at dusk and dawn. There is no such thing as America; only the plowing up, the plowing under. So that our lives are like all those yesterdays: before and after the orange and yellow squads of combines.

Because there is neither digression nor return, but merely cessation, we remembered to kiss goodbye. (And closed the doors on what?) Our habit of safety is no superstition —it is our only inheritance from those primal selfish proteins. Once on our way we perceived strangers everywhere, in everything terror. Had we abandoned what was probable for the barely possible? Yet it would have been wrong to protect ourselves. For later, in that standard and familiar rented American room, helpless in the net of the deepest embrace, we cried out to each other, spontaneously, "But who are you!"

THE GARDENER AT THIRTY

But I want you to understand
I find myself here to be known
Just as out back this piece of land
Waited ten years lying grassgrown

I myself an arm of no race
To stoop like that first settled man
And touch and probe this fallow place
To make it give me what it can

I revealed it like an old chest
Covered with books and webs of dust
Stripping it bare as my wife's breast
I pondered its promise and my lust

Tumultuous vegetables
Green striving, beans, corn, peas, it's true:
Nourished loves create our fables
Innocent powers, I've found you!

That was one of my morning dreams—
As if plenty were life, were all
To have to know to do clay's themes—
That was wisdom before the Fall

When light fails these mad weeds come through
My rows groan, deformed—ah poor patch
Like my nightmare I feel cold dew
As if I could bear it I'll watch

Mumbling monster rabbit who creeps
Full and silver magnificence:
My gardened human folly sleeps—
I'm here for my deliverance!

Haunting the lives of all you glide
Murdering owl, who know the worst,
Bring us truth wherever we hide
In hunger and hope we die cursed

Yet may we rest safe, and rest well
May I not hear the rabbit's scream
And, waking to dawn's mist, not tell
How I died waiting in my dream

HIGH SUMMER

Our lives are not renewable, yet we seek extinctions.
The effort needed to subdue and suppress that wise
fear, that monstrous tenacity of nature in us which
protects us from ourselves! What do we hope to discover
in these rare catastrophes? Further cycles of growth,
perhaps even to achieve the new capacities . . .

Is that why, though I'd promised nothing, I betrayed
you? Everywhere. In everything. As we ate and slept.
Even before our long spring began when the sun came
back with fresh light and winds out of the south breathed
upon the black sodden valley, recreating grass and the
blossoms as if from memory. It was all food. We were
promiscuous as bees. Yet I was always alone, aspiring
toward my own fulfillment. In our common acts of love
most of all. And you?

Leaves drooping coated with red dust. Confused by
the humid glare of an overcast afternoon sky, the
wild bees swarm irritably. The yellow hay has finally
stopped growing; waist-high it stands waiting the mower.
What was that long season of flowering but time's
metaphor? Errors ripen now, impersonal as our joys —
those accidents and brief coincidences in which matter
clings to matter like the touches of love. And the
seeds scattering, somewhere to overcome us: the
same things returning, inexorably full of themselves.
We should have known and expected it. But how?

Sitting by the road I watch the cars. Their passage
raises the clayey dust that chokes the leaves. We
have conquered this narrow strip of space in which
all are born. But what are those blank impassive
faces the people riding wear? They pretend to hide

our secret: that we go everywhere and come to nothing,
that even in the necessary and lucky exchanges of pollen
which preserve the world yesterday robs us of tomorrow.

So that we must destroy our lives because life has
destroyed us. Burning ways random as our unknown,
equivocal desires through time, that abyss of silence.
Imagine it, through time!

I can spot where the bees are at work in the hollow
trunk there finishing their graywalled, goldfilled
catacombs. The thinning coarsened foliage dies out,
stiffens, blackish-green. In expectation of the suns of
coming years, our cousins the living things have increased
themselves and multiplied. Now they begin to halt:
they will wait, without the vanity of hope: they will
survive their own deaths. But we, driving, driving,
do not slow—although when we are gone, in a month,
in a year, who can claim the strange harvest of this
incessant wintry assault on ourselves?

OCTOBER FLIES

One could not want a clearer season, when things age but
          do not grow, time fit for true meditations
the stained white house thrown up by summer's storm,
          stranded, abandoned on this crisp crackling
          backwash of brown leaves
all the birds asleep, huddled away from the frost owl, or
          flown whence their seasonal imperatives direct
and that gibbous moon, gleaned of color, dull as the rimed
          stooks, rocking on a porch of Prussian blue.

I, however, do not sit in the dark looking out at this
          transparency, this quasi-philosophical kodachrome,
but by a bright light ponder, considering next week's
          lectures, and think what I shall not say:
supposing Poe sober-sane, Hawthorne utterly mad, both,
          like myself, uxorious, in love with necessity
and up against it, its rigors and crotchets, etcetera, baffled
          by will and desire, baffled oh by right answers.

But it is very hard to think, because the flies have gone
     berserk, buzzing buzzing buzzing
they beat against my clean ceiling, where in consternation
     have they come from? and bash bash bash
indiscriminate, even for *Musca domestica*, beating about
     the bulb, caroming off the shade,
like spitballs whizzing, hopped-up like protons in a
     cyclotron, they crack against my face—and cling.

Ugh! it's not just the October chill has set this fly circus
     aswarm in crazy orbits—
their controls are shot, reckless senility misguides them,
     desperate, into these centrifugal throes:
unpredictable even to themselves, how can one stalk
     October flies! chaos! it is maddening!
yet, with calculated indirection, rather nonchalant,
     feigning purposelessness, I hunt these distractions
     down.

What I do, I clap hands over them as they sit—*Hai! Hai!*
     with a kind of Zen finesse—
they fall, stunned it would seem into thought, moreover
     still sufficiently alive for it,
wherefore, much against my better nature, I pull the
     brittle wings to calm the last agony
indeed to help them through their black October passage
     in dry meditation, as it were.

And for myself endeavor to give thanks for this their
     pestiferous excruciation (oh it is a sign!)
because, reckless, jumpy, despairingly unpredictable and
     buzzing beating bashing
I too make myself generally a nuisance unto God Who
     in this same night of Fall sits, alone,
pondering a *sensible* rhyme for His Own Name—to give
     thanks, I say, that, distracted, He clap not His
     Hands!

THE NIGHTMARE

You! whom the aged brandy does not burn
Cold lecher forcing technical boundaries
Dayblind, nightcalm, though bubs and bellies storm
Last judge of international anatomies
And you! sublime tricks breeding such quandaries
Smooth contraceptive eye, knee, lip, thigh
All contestants universal beauties
Quarrelling fuel, frantic for light

You! angels abroad weathering those abysms
Beyond me far as I transgress my natural
Having mounted beneath that hail of kisses
On perpetual stairs (dismal after the funeral)
And you too, her sonorities, thought infernal
You demand the bridge—the bridge, not seamen
And men for those hips undismayed though autumnal
Long hair, long laughter, and her cruel pleased mind

You, fluorescent in midnight blizzard! I see, I know!
Orbed bane striding through slush, spiritual beast
Rings of violet flaming as eyes, bare bleached brow
Hungry mouth of blue teeth, those sucked-out breasts
Naked ankles strapped on killing heels, such slut's taste
Beaked nose, clanging wrists, and hands bejewelled
Gaunt in black crêpe, a satin-sashed grim cocktail dress
You! ponderable there so terribly tall

Is it you? So, it's you! "Hag, accuse, bless!"
Silent on she comes pointing that harpy's manicure
The car stalls Drunk, I giggle, and retch "Blast!
O you! Hybrid! Roar, bitch! Blast! Make me—pure!"

MY GRANDMOTHER'S FUNERAL

She came across the seas steerage class
In her middle age, past childbearing,
Her husband sinking into dotage
Having sired two males upon her
And seven girls, none of them grateful
For her services as cook and char.

Her husband gone, at seventy-five
She had a hard stroke but was redeemed
By the young doctor who tapped her spine
And drew down with a pint of fluid
The troubling clot—so that she lived on
Blind in one eye, deafened, rather weak.

Another fifteen years she survived
Uselessly dimming in the poor corners
Of a household her last two daughters
Destroyed by their ignorant furies,
Lapsing incontinent, a burden
Had she known it even to herself.

She endured her perishing a week:
Bothered three days with what seemed a cold,
Pausing one night to let them bicker,
Who'd buy drugs? Who'd pay doctors? Her costs!
And slipping three days, slowly, slowly,
Toward those rattling rasping sighs, and death.

She was through yet she wasn't finished;
Consigned that hour to morticians,
Her hamper of flesh and bent old bones
Were zipped up in a green canvas sack
And bundled off—as they wept a tear
For mother, and two more for themselves.

On the next day at twelve-thirty sharp
She reappeared in Chapel C, West,
In a plain coffin of good grade oak,
To be viewed by mourners where she lay
Dressed in raw muslin, washed, and powdered,
And neatly stitched: she seemed someone else.

A short service for this old stranger
(The Fifth Commandment's Implications
Concerning Filial Obligations),
Delivered by a rented rabbi
In a spate of Buchenwald Yiddish,
Bad Hebrew, and peculiar English.

And then that sleek new Cadillac hearse
Driven by a rakish-capped chauffeur
Who wears aviator's sunglasses
And knows the fast route across the Bronx,
Over the Triborough Bridge to Queens,
Out expressways to the granite gates.

It's a glorious Spring afternoon;
Three robins dispute this hunting ground;
That man speaks his mangled speech, O God!
And the sandy loam is shoveled back,
Tactlessly neutral, filling the hole,
Making my brother's nose twitch with fear.

As the family turns toward the cars
He points at the Queens College buildings
Beyond the graveyard's south wall, and says,
"Next Fall when I'm admitted I'll drive
To campus over the Whitestone Bridge,"
And I say, "Taking *Humanities?*"

THREE POEMS

THE TECHNIQUE OF LOVE

Away with that tradition of wretched glory
Sustained by the memory of certain deep caresses,
That dream of lovers, and enemies — to have each other!

Wealth upon wealth! your charity impoverished me . . .
Was it right, was it good, to seek our humanity?
Alert, but wisely blind, like mirrors engaged: a nightmare!

Because your solicitudes gave me what I wished!
Oh my friend, may my generosities plunder you
Surfeits drown you, burn you, leave you to my death —

Forms emptied, momentary purities, each from each,
    unbound
And then, breakfasting on carbon, to find our equivalents,
Pleasures exquisite and black sentiment — obscure
    concentrations!

Yet to take, forget, take again and, unremembering, take
  once more!
I measure you with my fingers, and these estimations
  begin. Endless!
As if to understand, to accomplish ourselves, or become
  happy!

THE TECHNIQUE OF POWER

Poisoned, by our own lips! That exchange of
  eloquences . . .
Having worshipped too long in the same place—that
  radiance!
Our theory decayed into hard passions, perishing bits

Except the work to be done, nothing true can be known
Flesh parallel with flesh, ourselves merely the objects
        of force
As if love alone were precious! Now do you comprehend
  government?

Hence we joined, entering this silent momentum of things
Was it to resolve chastity that we opened our eyes in
  the dark,
Yielding tender as stoics to the mutualities of conquest?

All things are joyous but joy, whose kisses are blows
Compressed, heavy, durable—broken matters come to
  earth at last
Thus we grew human, having abandoned nothing but life

Yet, enlarged and preyed on by tomorrow, we will be
  hungrier
Rally the despairing fractions, command them to this
  new world
So that, iron ringing in our bones, we shall seem
  admirable killers!

THE TECHNIQUE OF LAUGHTER

You gave them all the dances, but came home with me
Then we bathed, and anointed each other with true lies
You showed me fields in the sea: I promised wild, honest
    tigers

To have torn ourselves away, lost them everywhere
    around us
Miracle! aspiring yet again and only to such nakedness!
They will say we lacked compassion, like survivors

Neither mine nor yours the courtesy of rotten states
Their archives burdened by the news of perpetual
    disasters
Absurd communities, cities rooted in our very hearts—
    gone!

Having destroyed ourselves and risen, ourselves once more
We drink this wine, resting content in the fruitful,
    bright mirage
Wanderers, come here! Green and gay, the world without
    hate or love

There, those shadows whirl grasping their possession,
    alive as ghosts!
But remember, remember we are real, it is no dream—
Soon we die, embracing and alone—remember we have
    lost nothing

P.S.

(For the PHI BETA KAPPA.)

A PROBLEM, hypothetical, in the form of a piercing di-
    lemma: *Surrender may be cheap, but life costs too
    much.*

A SOLUTION, hypothetical, in the form of a cornucopia spill-
    ing queries like random streams of lethal particles
    from which there is no shelter (except to exist in
    the saltmines).

*

AFTER SWITCHING the light out, but before dropping onto
bed (why not make this your setting-down exercise
for mind and heart and senses?), stand chilling
awhile at the window, contemplate the darkness
visible of that moving universe you are glad to
escape once more for your personal, uncontrollable
slumber, and consider what it asks: *Why is it there?
When will you be there? How can you get there?
And where* (should you miraculously be the very
one to guess the right answers—1, 2, 3!), *and
where will you be when you are there?*

COULD YOU, perhaps, have been studying the wrong sub-
jects all along? And were you, friends, inevitably
and necessarily misled by malicious gods (or
ghosts)? Or was it your ancestors' accidentally
accumulated and capriciously edited tables of
logarithm, law, latitude, organization which both
propelled and misguided you on this course? In
any case, given the right chance, if such there be,
can the antique weapons of the foundering vessel
somehow be turned against the strangers in our
midst, that is, against our heirs? Will you try?
Would it be any use to you to do so?

BUT MY FRIENDS, after having devoted yourselves with such
intensity to your lonely regiment of daily trotting
and push-ups, or alternatively, to mastering the
intricate systems of progressive jujitsu, which af-
fords security against superior antagonists, what
can you accomplish in the face-to-face, one-to-one
contest that eternity demands?

OR, NOT LOOKING THAT FAR AHEAD, what will account for the
liveliness of some old men and the stupidity of
others? Their glands? Is it money, diet, programmed-
exercises and regular check-ups? Is it meditation,
character, fate, or a subtle definite proportion of
each combined in a certain way? Could it be the
lingering yet remote effect of their first loves (**poor**

things! long since dwindled to putrid essences, like
rare cheese made from virgins' milk)? Is it maybe
climate, or even race? Can it depend on the quality
of the disciples who attend them? Perhaps it is
merely an illusion fostered by the imbecile selfish-
ness of all the rest of us, who are just the same for
better or worse almost quite as human although we
never realize it? Was there, in other words, a
woman to be searched for? Or, possibly, which
amounts to the same thing in the end, a woman to
be destroyed?

LOOK, to put it another way, *Suppose the Revolution is
coming?* If so, from what direction? And who is to
be executed? And is there never any possibility for
an honest reprieve? And when The Revolution
comes, what will it bring to the surface, extended
monstrously over the undulant dim waters like the
Great Pacific Squid basking in the starlight, more
real then than the scattered and hearsay reports of
its existence? Furthermore, which one of you will
be imaginative enough in his inescapable despair
and sufficiently brutalized by events to prepare The
Counterrevolution, and afterward The Counter-
Counterrevolution, and so on? And meanwhile
strong enough to endure forever the plangent
echoes of the bursting bombclusters and the how-
itzers firing in rotation, the muted, vibrant, thun-
derous idling of the enormous jets and the regular
convoys of trucks and tanks, and the printing
presses day and night pounding and rolling, the
staccato of loudspeakers shouting over them,
amplified unbearably, and indeed the peaceful
rumbling of the diesels of the field-turbines, and of
the tractors, the bulldozers, the graders and shovels
and cranes and rivetters and pavers, and then the
busses and typewriters and comptometers and
computers and cashregisters and airconditioners
and, mingled with it all, always, roocoocooing here
and there like courting mourningdoves, the machineguns, the machineguns . . . ? Is there any
substitute for the sound of the human voice?

THEREFORE, not to anticipate for you the unknown pleasures of white hair in retirement to the paradise of
patriarchal irresponsibility, let me ask you what is
bound to occur to you sometime, somewhere: in
the satiny stainless-steel, fluorescentlit and auto-
matic elevator rising and sinking morning or evening with that sickening glide in the sealed shaft,
or when, after jerking to a stop in the tunnel, the
engineless commuters' train waits, stale, then jerks
creeping ahead, or as the car is sidling forward in
suffocating endless traffic on the hazy parkways, or
sometime while you are manipulating the dials and
punching the keys in their marvellous sequences,
while listening patiently to the minutes of the
previous meeting and jotting down notes for the
minutes of the present meeting which will be read
at the next meeting (and glancing frequently, fur-
tively, at the selfwinding wristwatch), during the
sorting and filing of the week's correspondence, or
at the weighing-in of the luggage when en route to
conference sessions that will it is hoped occasion an
even greater flow of correspondence, or perhaps the
anxious yet fearfully excited and curious intake of
breath as you unfold the morning's incredible newspaper or later yank hurriedly at the recalcitrant
cigarette machine in the lobby for the necessary
second pack, or even while, during a rare free hour,
dialling the right number (you know *this* number
by heart!) but hanging up after the first buzz, your
palms moist and cold, or, in the dentist's waiting
room, staring fascinatedly at the fullpage fourcolor
photographs and wondering with envy and stultify-
ing dismay just where on earth those models were
posed with such insouciantly hieratic and meaning-
less attitudes — was it Alexandria, Cuzco, Pompeii?
under the Sphinx, in Bombay, Rio de Janiero,
Teheran, Odessa, St. Peter's Square, at the Lincoln
Memorial or Nassau, under St. Paul's dome, in
Bangkok, Nome, Alaska, on Hawaii's black-sand
beach, Wall Street or San Diego or the Free-
Market of Hongkong, Singapore, Montreal, Copen-
hagen, the Fjords, and so forth . . . places, places,

perpetual recollections of the geography of adver-
tising! or are they actually, you know, really only
facsimiles of sunlight faked up against the studio
wall with artificial architecture and the false luxury
of the patina or ancient props which makes anything authentic—or, some other time altogether,
between the locker-room and the barbeque pit,
maybe while ruminatively shaking the last two
spoons of BromoSeltzer out of the famous blue-
glass bottle, or, late again for the party and rum-
maging for the missing cufflink, or while waxing the
fishline in the springtime (in autumn, greasing the
heavy boots, also sorting the cartridges, or, it might
well be, slumping dazed in the barberchair without your glasses and unable to see what's been done,
or mulling the odds changing constantly up there on
the board as the line moves up, too easily, toward
the betting window, or, after the last drink, fum-
bling for the elusive hatcheck, or sometime between the fantastic hors d'oeuvres and the terrified
glances of hostess and host as the evening is chewed
relentlessly and swallowed down and drowned in
boredom boredom boredom! during, that is to
suggest, that inevitable prolonged moment when
your life ascends irretrievably to the outer cold
and falls into the fixed trajectory of the permanent
orbit, and reality retreats whirling below and behind, its weight dragging at you with a force of 5 to
15 G's and pressing the multiplied tons of your own
existence against the chest like the final remorse,
and, as you thence become separated once and forever from your own self, able to view it all and yet
unable to distinguish anything whatsoever in its
particular homely detail (unless by means of special
lenses which unfortunately will reveal far too
much): when, in short, in short it is finally too late
and history is all there is left to you, and illumina-
tion comes out of the infinite black depth and you
know that there was no way to have known that
what you somehow knew, somehow knew, was
really accurate and true . . . and then it is that
that appalling dream suddenly comes back, that

dream which woke you even from the heavy sleep-
ing arms of your beloved . . .

Blue and red and white flames glinting and
glaring on the midnight's horizon like silent
slow explosions: a couple of old dolls flung,
seeming grotesquely alive, in the corner of
the dusty room, words and phrases uttered
in the air, raucous wild syllables breaking out
of the cackles and growls, sentences running
over into threats and moans and futile sup-
plications—as if one had suddenly but ir-
revocably abandoned to itself the world one
had made . . . do you comprehend this?
one's own created world! . . . which had
seemed so bad, so ugly and untrue—but
perhaps (though how was one to believe it?)
only because it was one's own?

Barbara Guest

LES RÉALITÉS

It's raining today and I'm reading about pharmacies
     in Paris.
Yesterday I took the autumn walk, known in May as
     lovers' walk.
Because I was overwhelmed by trees (the path from the
     playhouse
leads into a grove and beyond are the gravestones),
squirrels and new mold it is a good thing today
to read about second-class pharmacies where
mortar and plastic goods disturb death a little
and life more. It is as if perpetual rain
fell on those drugstores making the mosaic brighter,
as if entering those doors one's tears
were cleaner.

     As if I had just
left you and was looking for a new shade of powder
orchidée, ambre, rosé, one very clarified and true
to its owner, one that in a mirror
would pass for real and yet when your hand falls upon it
(as it can) changes into a stone or flower of the will
and triumphs as a natural thing,
     as this pharmacy
turns our desire into medicines and revokes the rain.

THE HERO LEAVES HIS SHIP

I wonder if this new reality is going to destroy me.
There under the leaves a loaf
The brick wall on it someone has put bananas
The bricks have come loose under the weight,
What a precarious architecture these apartments,
As giants once in a garden. Dear roots
Your slivers repair my throat when anguish
commences to heat and glow.

From the water
A roar. The sea has its own strong wrist
The green turf is made of shells
      it is new.

     I am about to use my voice
Why am I afraid that salty wing
Flying over a real hearth will stop me?

     Yesterday the yellow
Tokening clouds. I said 'no' to my burden,
The shrub planted on my shoulders. When snow
Falls or in rain, birds gather there
In the short evergreen. They repeat their disastrous
Beckoning songs as if the earth
Were rich and many warriors coming out of it,
As if the calm was blue, one sky over
A shore and the tide welcoming a fleet
Bronzed and strong as breakers,

     Their limbs in this light
Fused of sand and wave are lifted once
Then sunk under aquamarine, the phosphorous.

Afterwards this soundless bay,
Gulls fly over it. The dark is mixed
With wings. I ask if that house is real,
If geese drink at the pond, if the goatherd takes
To the mountain, if the couple love and sup,

     I cross the elemental stations
from windy field to still close. Good night I go
      to my bed.
This roof will hold me. Outside the gods survive.

SADNESS

We were walking down a narrow street.
It was late autumn. In my hotel room
the steam heat had been turned on. In the office
buildings, in the boutiques, coal was lit.

That morning I had been standing at the window
looking out on the Tuileries. I had been crying
because the yellow tulips were gone and all the children
were wearing thin coats. I felt an embarrassing pain
distributed over my arms which were powerless
to order the leaves to blossom or the old women
on the stairs to buy shoes to cover their feet.

Then you took my hand. You told me that love
was a sudden disturbance of the nerve ends
that startled the fibres and made them new
again. You quoted a song about a man running
by the sea who drew into his lungs the air
that had several times been around the world.

A speck of coal dust floated down and settled on my
    lapel.
Quickly with your free hand you rubbed out the spot.
Yet do you know I shall carry always
that blemish on my breast?

BELGRAVIA

I am in love with a man
Who is more fond of his own house
Than many interiors which are, of course, less unique,
But more constructed to the usual sensibility,
Yet unlike those rooms in which he lives
Cannot be filled with crystal objects.

These are embroidered chairs
Made in Berlin to look like cane, very round
And light which do not break, but bend
Ever so slightly, and rock at twilight as the cradle
Rocks itself if given a slight push and a small
Tune can be heard when several of the branches creak.

Many rooms are in his house
And they can all be used for exercise.
There are mileposts cut into the marble,
A block, ten blocks, a mile

For the one who walks here always thinking,
Who finds a meaning at the end of a mile
And wishes to entomb his discoveries.

I am in love with a man
Who knows himself better than my youth,
My experience or my ability
Trained now to reflect his face
As rims reflect their glasses,
Or as mirrors, filigreed as several European
Capitals have regarded their past
Of which he is the living representative,
Who alone is nervous with history.

I am in love with a man
In this open house of windows,
Locks and balconies,
This man who reflects and considers
The brokenhearted bears who tumble in the leaves.

In the garden which thus has escaped all intruders
There when benches are placed
Side by side, watching separate entrances,
As one might plan an audience
That cannot refrain from turning ever so little
In other directions and witnessing
The completion of itself as seen from all sides,

I am in love with him
Who only among the invited hastens my speech.

THE FIRST OF MAY

My eye cannot turn toward you
Night
because it has Day watching.

(A spoon heated over the fire,
a cup with milk in it
shadows at its brim.)

I would like to go for a walk
in the dark
without moonbeams

down that path of mushrooms
in my nightdress
without shoes.

I would like to sit under your wall
and you fortify me
as you did once on the road,
a stranger.

I would like to steal
and take it to you.

I would like to go to a hotel
with you.

Turn out the lights!

Your arms, I feel them,
your eyes, I cannot see them.

Day is watching me
from over the transom.

Day whose light is blinding me,
as lightning on the firebreak
of a mountain,

who brings me a quail
caught in the smoldering underbrush

where the smell is of yucca
and sage.

Day brings me this bird.

I must go and feed it
with milk from the cup,
a few drops on the spoon.

The sirens are screaming
in the streets.
It is an order to take cover.
And I, I
must bring this bird to shelter.

I must not be caught out
in the night
unless I am willing

to give you up Day forever,
when I join the guerrillas,

who would like my cup
and spoon,

who would roast my bird
and eat it.

WAVE

i

And   preparing a net
                 Wave

whose arm is green
                 your
half-wayness I, too, would meet you there

                 in foam

                 Borders

the rip slices   turns   backwards
swimmers this treachery is cast by mirrors
once in profile only this multiplied

                 the arrow backstroke sent to bliss

we cry deepest and turn not daring to spy

full-face on ocean crest that carries on

　　　　　　on

space now azure fullest where the depth

is danger
　　　　　　　long roll
Again   the ride

　　　　　　　　　And equinoctial plunge

it dares   beach   the   horizon

　　　　　　with you

　　　　　　　　wailings
(that drift shrieks at low tide)

　　　　　　bubbling

the loose and soggy shelf

　　　　　　Bell

ii

the eye tolls as burnished as Bell
on coral the wave breaks or here
cold zone of equal blue and grey

　　　　　　Triton's throng appears

　　　　　　　　where zephyrs
cast skyward by the spume glance down
on islands of the deep mermaids
we'll never see   or hear   yet each

wave rolling brings in brightest
phosphorescence their hair

　　　　　　a lyre

sweet voice of brine

                      other secrets

in the tease and stress of wave song

                        Sun

multipowered it brushes

thins and splays

                        burns

wild-lidded over foam   in air   to touch

                      Remembering the violence
we turn on house pillow and let
dolphins surmise us (dreams) the lap
of shore water enter our heads as ponds
forced from sea are inlets, we are
islets become soft   become grassy
turning   swaying   to each and yet

                  the angry

                  it calls

Noon

    the crab walks

Night
    small fish

Rock and dawn

    Fog

iii

I would walk from this porch to your farthest

                do I dare

Lights without you the house is ghosty
$\qquad$ the pier is broken
$\qquad$ its points are webbed

cricket and bird song about   alas

$\quad$ until morning   the great sea and ledge

from which pines such low soundings   pines

that are green   and sea that is swelling

sea whose earth is sandy who in sleep

$\quad$ changes as the pilot arm beckons

the arm we lie on shifts

$\qquad$ early the stir

to cease from night close   to begin

to gather   to fall   as Wave

$\qquad$ Bountiful and Bare

"EVERYTHING IN THE AIR IS A BIRD"

Jorge Guillen

$\quad$ It is
$\quad$ yet almost
$\quad$ I do not see it.

$\quad$ Obscured so many days
$\quad$ by dark thunder
$\quad$ many nights of sealed windows
$\quad$ when the draughts
$\quad$ glide under the door
$\quad$ their fingers reach my throat
$\quad$ my dreams are stifled
$\quad$ my dreams are of dust and felt.

The buildings praised by contractors
they do not let me see it.
Those skyscrapers someone is proud of,
who has written,
"Up there is sunlight and snow,"

Yet I do not hear that voice
those wings do not whir.

I hear eight million people
I hear water running in sinks
I see signs, but they are not symbols.

The pavement is tough under my feet
birds do not feed at its rivers
water flows into gutters
without a roar,
without a single sentence.

This unbearable noise
of no sibilants
this rake passing over burned lots
where the rubble is heaped
into a crevasse
where the crevasse
becomes an abyss.

Monumental monuments of glass.

Close your eyes again
it is necessary
that the seasons
poach your eyelids

That they move over you their wings
they fan the still air
into an awakening

That is new
that is fresh

Where the cranes and the crocodiles
find a mudbank
and rocks for the antelopes

Lower your altitudes
that no longer in the city
you pass as a stranger with thirst

who finds each breath
difficult.

No more in the city block
to find these barriers
the wind cannot surmount.

The air whistles in the caverns
it moans where it is stunned.

I hate these brass knuckles
rapping eternally rapping

when the air is free

the air is a bird.

John Hollander

WHEN ALL OF THEM RAN OFF

When all of them ran off, laughing, over
    the dunes, and up along the high
      spine of the island,
      three miles back home, through
tangles of brush and the sweeps of broom, green
          broom.
      silent winds three miles above us
        blew
    white clouds away from the sun
      and all the beach gleamed,
      cries of the flying
gulls dispersed into the lapping of the
        tired
      water. From above,
    the cove must have seemed a shallow
    horseshoe, opening out toward the
variable sea, implying all that
      possibility
      lying outside it;
    from where we were it showed only
    its idiotically blank,
    bright face, and we were suddenly
      really alone, and
      even the sheep who
had wandered almost to the beach's edge
before had vanished over the green hill.

    Going inside the cottage was
    sillier even than staying
      out
here in the first place: the old newspapers
      piled on the sighing
      and faded bedspreads
were recent enough to be sinister,
and the wind rattled the windows, and dark
      gray sand lay like dust

        in the bottoms of pieces of white, cracked
                ironware, lying
on corners of tables in dimming rooms.

Before we knew it, the water
            had gloomed into gray;
            inside, the light was
            very, very faint,
        outside, it was less dark, though it
            might have been night, and
        we waited twenty minutes more
to be picked up, staring across at the dark
                boat
            silently plying
            toward us, and even
                then,
before, the water sloshing cold
and dead about our ankles, we
            finally contrived to
                move
            into the chilling,
            sad, September night.

SLEPYNGE LONG IN GREET QUIETE IS EEK A
GREET NORICE TO LECCHERIE

for Norman and Midge

Sunk earlier in the silence of grey cashmere
    Muffler, the clock had only grown alarmed
After my three long burials in the sweet, cool
    Fields of sheet; and appalled after the huge
And sudden drumlin stood up in the blanket, Big
    Ben held up both his hands, surrendered and
Stopped. I slept on, turned, snorted, flushed, formed
        new prairies,
    Opened a diffident eye, blinked, and felt
Impingements of the cold upon the frosty eye
    My room turned toward the shining sun, new high
Above the harsh, cold fields of sleet outside. Around
    The room my mirror saw no evil, swung
Upward, reflecting white permissive fields of ceiling,

Its gaze averted from me and from keys
(One missing), change, two hankies, scurfy comb and
    things
Spread on the mote-collecting bureau top
Below. I turned again, and subterranean
    Stiffening made its mark outside, and when
There seemed no help for it, the steps outside the door
    Quickened, and tapping (muffled by what turned
Out in a moment to be a bright red mitten) fell
    Onto the silent hills my knees made, snow
Shivered, and, hushed, fell down outside the glass.
        Then in
    She came and February's color spoke
Out of her face less loudly than the mittens but
    More sweetly, till she fell across my meadow
(Strawberries scattered on the snow) and then I was
    Asleep again, unbelievable fields
Moving beneath my feet, the chase always moving
    Faster and farther, then in the cedar hedge
Finishing. As the window tore up half a foot
    The cold ripped through the fields of fleet pursuit,
Licked at my nose, then went to earth beside the wedge
    Of shoulder that the bedclothes left exposed.
I was awake by then. Hard on the heels of cold,
    She harried it across the room; her shoulders
Were clutched in opposite hands, her elbows rustled
    Against the white electric fields of slip
That lay quite cold against her. "Off with it then,
        silly!"
    The icy blast insisted, but the while
She ran up to the bed and rested one thin, buff
    Knee against the pillow, seizing a piece
Of smooth, white acreage below each arm with crossed
    Hands, dragging it upward, scraping nervous
Skin just beneath it, from the street below a harsher
    Scraping subdued that whisper of how cold she was.
Gray fields of slop below were being cleared away
    And wet, black sidewalks glistened underfoot.
—Oh, all that enterprise outside should probably
    Have urged us out into the waking world,
Over the shiny fields of slippery park, perhaps,
    Down to the Zoo ("Hello, Yak") or along

Apartment house-lined chasms to the oldest wing
　　Of the museum, to try to glimpse again
The failing winter light, falling across glass cases
　　Up in the dim, high room that frightened us
Long ago as children. All that industrious clearing-
　　Away of snow could call us out to no
Activities, however, and I only reached
　　Out for the taut, white band of pants that gripped
Her skin for cold and drew her towards me by it. How
　　The ice cold Karakorums that the sheet
Covered with snow resisted her ascent along
　　The bed's chill length! How valiantly she crept
Over the shifting fields of steep traverse beneath her!
　　Finally, near frozen, at the summit she
Found haven, drew the covers up, popped in, and lay
　　Beside me, shivering with no cold now,
But with the heat of what was happening, as we
　　Faced the last, high, white summit that loomed up
Before us both. And then there was no help for it
　　Again, and there we were and there it was,
And so we had to climb it, cold winds singing always
　　About our heads, until we wept and died
And lay there freezing slowly in the dying light
　　With which the changing world outside peeped in.

BY THE SEA

Joe, mach die Musik von damals nach!

The dark, gray receding tide uncovers
New reaches of white sand; and underfoot
Dry bony driftwood moves into the shade,
　　　Growing as cold as
　　　The sparrow-colored
Cliffs that hover above the beach to mark
The rooted boundaries beyond all which
Nothing made of the sea may pass. The flying
　　　Onshore winds only
　　　Flap through an awning

Over the empty beach house. The sun becomes
Paler than one could believe. The treachery
Of memory is probably no deeper now
    Than it is ever;
    But when, toward evening,
Summer shivers into covering darkness,
Spreading no particular season's chill
Down the beach, older remembered images
    Invade the prospect.
    Like the preposterous

Youngsters who come prancing over the sand,
Waiting for sundown on the hard, cold beach
To send them groping for each other's furry
    Parts, in the blackness
    Of sandy blankets,
Handling the loneliness, the only *Angst*
Each has ever known, in the only ways
Occurring to them, we ourselves expend
    Passion on peeping
    (at seascapes, perhaps)

Or on grabbing a feel of this night air
Nearly as nervously as they. Their rubbish,
Found, at morning, in pools among the rocks
    Manages somehow
    To hold a simple
Bare innocence always (white, floating relics
Of hurried ceremonies, looking fairly
Like the dead blowfish that meander round them)
    Remaining harmless;
    While all the horrid

Nonsense of moments we have left behind
Drifts up onto the shores of consciousness
And waits to betray us. Even this stark scene
    Robbed of its being
    By other beaches,
Winds, sunsets, tides, our own touches of darkness,
Senseless, gauche, and inconsiderate gifts
Given us by what once we were, and baited
    With what, in all traps,
    Seems most attractive,

Even this strange new beach becomes, beclouded
By unforgetting eyes, one of the Good
Old Places. And the roaring of the sand's edge,
    Tunditur unda,
      Thundering under
High, loud breakers blasting the uneven
Tides of silence, alternating with windy
Pianissimi that whimper through the cold,
    Sighing to cadence,
      Is quickly cuddled

By pampering recollection, in whose embrace
All the wild music is drowned in the Old Song
With the embarrassing title that is lodged
    Deep in our hearing.
      All its heaving,
Precious, banal progressions work toward damping
Everything that purports to be musical.
The stodgiest tune will have its aftermath
    (When once forgotten,
      Or, like the gods of

A place one has been banished from, remembered
In all despite of better judgment) always
Remaining, like the flapping of the wind,
    Tumbling of breakers,
      The gray terns' braying,
Somehow prior to other singing. Faced
With waves, surrounded by sand, tangled in tall
Bundles of crab grass, we are marooned in strains
    And chords of habit
      Because of having

Faced other beaches, if only remembered
Faintly as being dreamt of, mediating
Between us and the scene before us, fading
    Softly to darkness.

DIGGING IT OUT

The icicle finger of death, aimed
At the heart always, melts in the sun
But here at night, now with the porchlight
Spilling over the steps, making snow
More marmoreal than the moon could,
It grows longer and, as it lengthens,
Sharpens. All along the street cars are
Swallowed up in the sarcophagus
Mounds, and digging out had better start
Now, before the impulse to work dies,
Frozen into neither terror nor
Indifference, but a cold longing
For sleep. After a few shovelfuls,
Chopped, pushed, then stuck in a hard white fudge,
Temples pound; the wind scrapes icily
Against the beard of sweat already
Forming underneath most of my face,
And halting for a moment's only
Faltering, never resting. There is
Only freezing here, no real melting
While the thickening silence slows up
The motion of the very smallest
Bits of feeling, even.
                              Getting back
To digging's easier than stopping.
Getting back to the unnerving snow
Seems safer than waiting while the rush
Of blood inside one somewhere, crazed by
The shapes one has allowed his life to
Take, throbs, throbs and threatens. If my heart
Attack itself here in the whitened
Street, would there be bulges and the sound
Of hoofbeats thumping on a hard-packed,
Shiny road of snow? Or is that great
Onset of silences itself a
Great white silence? The crunching of wet
Snow around my knees seems louder, now
That the noises of the fear and what the
Fear is of are louder too, and in
The presence of such sounding depths of

Terror, it is harder than ever
To believe what I have always heard:
That it feels at first like spasms of
Indigestion. The thought, as one shoves
Scrapingly at the snow that always
Seems to happen to things and places
That have been arranged just so, the thought
Of being able to wonder if
Something I'd eaten had disagreed
With me, the while waiting to die, is
Ridiculous. "Was it something I
felt?" "Something I knew?" "Something I was?"
Seem more the kind of thing that one might
Wonder about, smiling mildly, as
He fell gently no great distance to
The cushioning world that he had dug.
Silently—for to call out something
In this snow would be to bury it.
And heavily, for the weight of self
Is more, perhaps at the end, than can
Be borne.

        No, it is only now, as
I urge the bending blade beneath a
Snow-packed tire for what I know can
Not be the last time that I whimper:
I hate having to own a car; I
Don't want to dig it out of senseless
Snow; I don't want to have to die, snow
Or no snow. As the wind blows up a
Little, fine, white powders are sprinkled
Across the clear windshield. Down along
The street a rustle of no leaves comes
From somewhere. And as I realize
What rest is, pause, and start in on a
New corner, I seem to know that there
Is no such thing as overtaxing,
That digging snow is a rhythm, like
Breathing, loving and waiting for night
To end or, much the same, to begin.